SHARPENING
with
WATERSTONES

SHARPENING
with
WATERSTONES

A PERFECT EDGE IN 60 SECONDS

Ian Kirby

CAMBIUM PRESS
Newtown, CT USA

Sharpening with Waterstones

ISBN 0-9643999-3-8

First printing: March 1998
Printed in the United States of America

Published by
Cambium Press
PO Box 909
Bethel, CT 06801
tel 203-426-6481 fax 203-426-0722
email CAMBIUMBOOKS.COM

Distributed to the book trade by
Lyons Press
31 W. 21st St.
New York NY 10010
tel 212-620-9580 fax 212-929-1836

**Library of Congress
Cataloging-in-Publication Data**
Kirby, Ian J., 1932-
    Sharpening with waterstones : a perfect
edge in 60 seconds / Ian Kirby.
        p.   cm.
    Includes index.
    ISBN 0-9643999-3-8 (pbk.)
    1. Woodworking tools--Maintenance
and repair.   2. Sharpening of tools.
3. Grinding wheels.   I. Title
TT186.K58 1998
621.9'3'--dc21   98-2860
                                        CIP

CONTENTS

CHAPTER 1

A perfect edge in 60 seconds

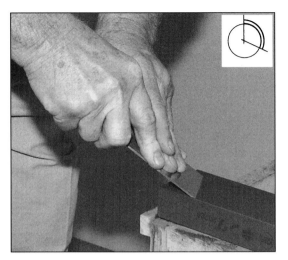

1. Take the blade out of the plane and remove the cap iron.

2. Sharpen the edge on the medium stone: 20 seconds.

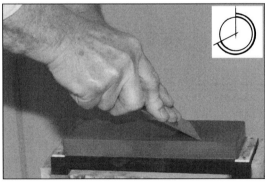

3. Refine the edge on the fine stone: 20 seconds.

4. Back off on the fine stone: 10 seconds.

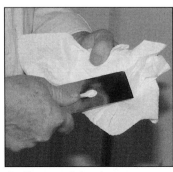

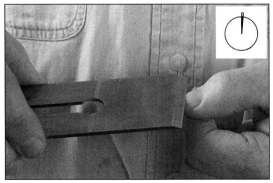

5. Clean and dry the blade: 5 seconds.

6. Check for sharp: 5 seconds.

Anybody can learn how to sharpen planes, chisels, carving tools, and knives. It is simply a matter of learning what to do and when to do it. The people who make and sell honing gadgets have turned sharpening into a kind of voodoo, but there are no magic tricks. You can learn how to do it, and once you have done so, the skill is yours to keep.

We've tried all the sharpening methods, systems and gizmos on the market. We've settled on the system detailed in this book as the quickest, cheapest and most effective one out there. It goes like this:

grind with a soft, slow-running wheel,
sharpen the cutting edge on a medium waterstone,
refine the cutting edge on a fine waterstone,
polish the flat back face on a fine waterstone.

This method is quick, straightforward to learn, and easy on your wallet. And you get superb results, as you can see in the plane-iron demonstration on these two pages.

7. Replace the cap iron.   *8. Reassemble and adjust the cap iron and blade.*

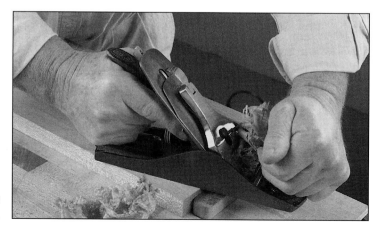

9. You're back to work.

What is sharp?

The sharp edge on a plane or chisel is the result of two smooth metal surfaces meeting at an angle of 35 degrees.

How smooth is smooth?

Smooth metal reflects light like a mirror.

**The smoother the surface,
the sharper the edge,
and the longer it will stay sharp.**

Here's why. When you rub a blade on a sharpening stone, the abrasive grit scores the metal, wearing it away. The grit leaves tiny grooves in the metal. Magnified, the grooves would be like a steak knife, though irregular and random, so the meeting surfaces would look like the teeth on a saw. Such an edge would cut tomatoes, but when pushed through wood, the fine teeth quickly break off, leaving the edge flat and thick. It is blunt.

The fine sharpening stone wears the grooves down to mirror smoothness, so the metal no longer looks like a steak knife. There are no teeth—the edge is continuous. So, two polished faces meet in a very sharp edge which won't break down in the wood. A polished edge is not only sharp, it also will stay sharp longer than a rough edge.

New tools are not sharp when you receive them from the store. They probably have been ground to an angle near 35 degrees, but the metal is not smooth. Really smooth metal reflects light like a mirror. You have to create this smoothness for yourself.

The back face of the blade has to be as smooth and bright as the sharpening bevel. Check it with a magnifying glass.

Checking for sharp

By sight

Look straight at the edge, with light coming over your shoulder. If it is dull, you will see a thin line of light reflected from the dull edge. If it is sharp, you won't be able to see a line of the light because there's no flat surface to reflect it. To get a better view, look at the edge with a magnifying glass.

"SHARP" IS TWO FLAT, MIRROR-SMOOTH SURFACES MEETING AT A 35-DEGREE ANGLE.

By touch

Test the edge against your thumbnail, as shown in the photo. This is an ancient method used by silver engravers.

Set the edge against the flat of your nail and slowly lower the angle between tool and nail. A sharp edge will catch the nail and stick at any elevation. You won't cut yourself because you don't push the edge. Just set the edge on the nail without any force or pressure. Try the same test with a dull edge before you sharpen it — it slides all over the place.

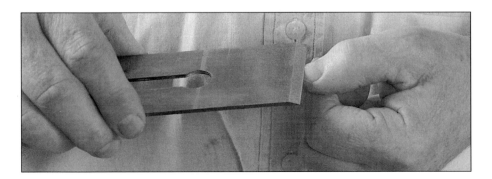

Three surfaces

On woodworking planes and chisels, the sharp edge arises at the intersection of two surfaces: the **back face** of the blade and the **sharpening bevel**. These two surfaces meet at an angle of 30 to 35 degrees.

Because of the way we sharpen tools, you're also concerned with a third surface, the **grinding bevel**. The grinding bevel speeds up the act of sharpening, but it is not part of the sharp edge itself.

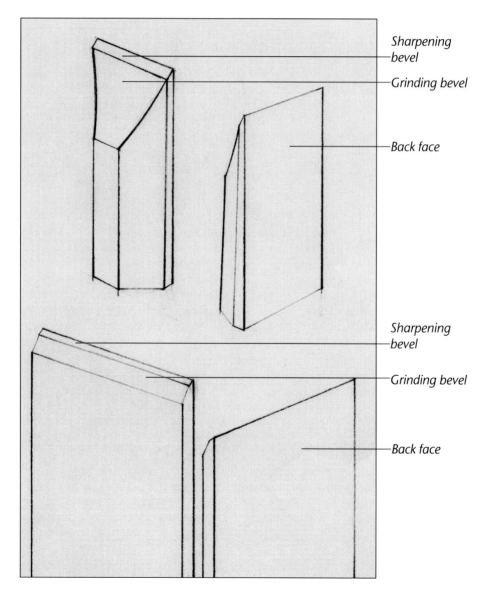

Sharpening bevel

Grinding bevel

Back face

Sharpening bevel

Grinding bevel

Back face

The sharpening bevel

The sharpening bevel has to be flat, and polished mirror bright. It has the same qualities as the back face of the blade, because the sharp edge arises at the intersection of the two faces.

The sharpening bevel and the back face meet at an angle of about 35 degrees on planes, 30 degrees on chisels. **The sharpening angle is steeper than the grinding angle**, though the precise number of degrees is a matter of preference and experience. There's more about the sharpening angle on *page 75* and *page 80.*

The flat back face

When you buy a new woodworking tool, the first thing to do is prepare the back face of the blade. It has to be dead flat, right up to the cutting edge, and it has to be as smooth as a mirror. Flatten it on a coarse waterstone, then polish it on the two finer stones you'll use for sharpening.

Get the back face flat once and you'll never have to do it again.

All you have to do is polish it each time you sharpen, in a quick maneuver called "backing off." There's more detail about the technique of flattening on *page 64.*

The grinding bevel

The grinding bevel has only one purpose: **it makes sharpening faster**. It's what allows you to sharpen a blade in 60 seconds or less. Without a grinding bevel you'd have to remove ten times as much metal at each sharpening, which would take too long and would destroy your sharpening stones. It would also be very rough on your hands and body. The grinding bevel is always at an angle of 25 degrees to the back face, on both planes and chisels.

Microbevel - *a misleading term*

The term "microbevel" has crept into magazine articles and books about sharpening. The term has been used in a variety of confusing ways. There is only the sharpening bevel and the grinding bevel, and the one that cuts is the sharpening bevel, no matter how "micro" you make it.

Sharp planes

The payback from sharp tools is superb results at the workbench. The woodworking plane does three operations.

The plane brings wood precisely to size.
It makes a flat surface.
It creates a smooth surface, ready to finish.

The plane can produce these results working with the grain, across the grain, and on end grain.
A sharp plane makes a distinctive singing sound as it slices through the wood. The sharp sing of the plane falls off after ten or twenty shavings, but the sound of cutting remains crisp. As the tool becomes blunt, the sound becomes dull and flat. You can tell by the sound and the feel when it is time to pause and resharpen.

Sharp chisels

A 1-inch chisel will cut across the corner of hard oak with ease, leaving a surface that can't be improved by any other tool or procedure.

A sharp plane glides easily through end-grain.

The plane leaves a clean and smooth surface.

A sharp chisel slices cleanly through the end-grain of the hardest wood.

Finishing straight from the plane

If the grain of the wood is straight and aligned just right — and it's surprising how often this is so — you can apply a finish directly after planing. Plane to remove the machine marks. Feel the wood. It will be astonishingly smooth. The fibers have been cleanly cut. No other method of finishing can create such a bright and crisp smoothness. Sanding or scraping will only degrade the surface.

Not all wood is perfect. Sometimes the best wood has a spot where the grain twists and the fibers lift out of the surface. Plane the wood, then sand the difficult area with fine sandpaper, 200 grit and then 320 grit.

Even the most difficult wood with the wildest grain can be tamed with a sharp plane. The technique is to plane across the grain with the blade set fine. The sharper the blade and the finer the cut, the smoother the surface. The cut can be so fine that you can begin sanding with 320-grit paper. However, once you sand, you can't go back to planing, because the residual abrasive left on the wood will blunt the edge of the blade in just a couple of strokes. No matter how awkward the wood grain, planing by hand remains the fastest, easiest path to a finished surface.

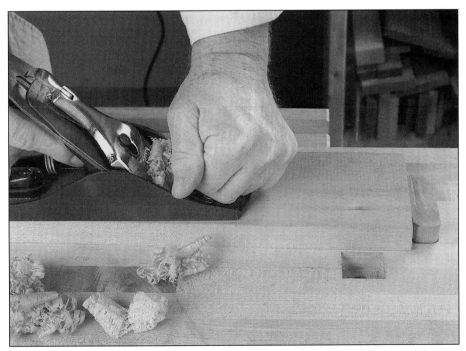

The plane peels a crisp shaving off the long-grain surface of the wood, leaving a lustrous gleam behind.

Your sharpening equipment

Your investment in equipment for keeping sharp tools always at hand is about $200. This includes all the gear you need, plus materials for construction of two work stations, one for grinding and one for sharpening. There are no gizmos to add, no upgrades to buy. This equipment will last the rest of your life.

What you need

Grinding station

Grinder. Slow-running: 1800 RPM. Expect to pay $80 $100. *Page 16.*
Grinding wheel. 6 inch dia. by 3/4 inch wide, soft, cool-running, pink or white. Expect to pay about $25. *Page 18*
Tool rest. Shop made. *Page 27.*
Tool holders. Shop made. *Page 28 to 35.*
Wheel dresser. Carborundum, Crystolon or diamond. *Page 43.*
Safety goggles. *Page 23.*

Sharpening station

Sharpening bench. Shop made. *Page 56.*

Waterstones. Coarse, medium, and fine. Expect to pay $75 to $90 for all three. *Page 46.*

Water bucket and plastic squeeze bottle.

Plate glass, 12 x 12, 1/4 inch thick.

Wet-dry sandpaper, 100 grit

Angle gauge. Shop-made from wooden block. *Page 75.*

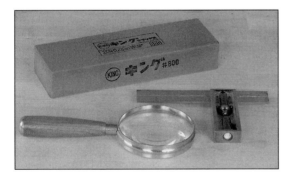

It's helpful to have

800-grit stone.

Magnifying glass, 4x, or 10x hand lens.

Machinist's try square, 4 inch.

Paper towels.

You don't need

Grinder tool rest. Manufactured tool rests are over-elaborated, expensive, and quickly ruined by the grit the wheel throws off. The simple bar-style rest shown on page 26 and 27 is safe, inexpensive, long-lasting and does a great job.

Angle guide or honing guide. Sharpening is a simple skill. Manufactured guides themselves require learning yet another new skill in order to use them. The manufactured guide deprives you of tactile feedback and precise control, and some styles will damage your waterstones.

CHAPTER 2

Grinders and grinding wheels

The edge of any steel cutting tool can be shaped by removing metal with a grinding wheel.

Grinding is an abrasive process that generates heat. Heat changes steel. Too much heat draws the temper from the metal, making it too soft to hold an edge. You can see the effect of heat as the oxidation colors appear on the steel and change as it gets hotter. The instant the steel's color changes from silver to straw or blue or purple, it's too late. By the time you see the colors, the steel's temper has already been drawn.

There are two ways to deal with heat: cool the steel while it's being ground, or avoid overheating in the first place. While the steel could be cooled with a spray of water or oil, it's complicated to achieve. The second solution is better: avoid overheating. This requires three things:

a slow-speed grinder,
a soft, coarse wheel,
a light touch.

Shopping for a grinder

There are many types of grinders on the market. For wood-working tools you need what's called a 6-inch grinder, which takes a 6-inch-diameter wheel. The key difference is running speed. Most grinders run around 3600 RPM, but some run at 1800 RPM. For woodworking tools, you need the slower machine. The speed will always be marked on the motor plate.

Grinders usually come with grey carborundum wheels, which are not the best thing for woodworking tools, because they run too hot. So, along with the grinder you must also buy the correct wheel. You can also mount a variety of felt buffs, wire brushes and polishing mops on the grinder's mandrel, for other operations.

Woodworking catalogs offer a variety of wet-dry grinding and sharpening systems that cost $300 or even more. If you have already bought one, you will be able to get excellent results with it. However, unless you are going into the sharp-ening business, you don't need to spend that $300. All you need is an inexpensive bench-top grinder that runs at a slow speed, and it will cost between $80 and $100.

Even if you already have a 3400 to 3600-RPM bench grinder, don't try to make do with it. The motor plate may show how to rewire it for a slower speed, and if so, do so. Otherwise, buy a new, slow-speed grinder. You'll recover the additional investment by not damaging your tools.

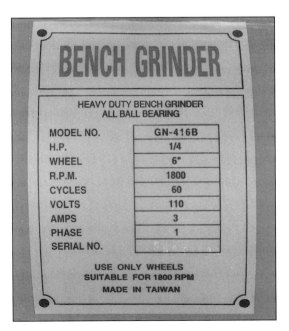

The motor plate lists the grinder's specifications, including its running speed. This grinder, which cost $80, runs at 1800 RPM.

Grinding wheel

The right wheel won't burn the steel

A grinding wheel contains three things:

abrasive grit, the particles that cut the steel;
the bond that holds the abrasive grit in place;
air spaces within the matrix of grit and bond.

Grinding wheels are vitreous, which means they are made by a firing process that sets the abrasive grit in a glasslike but porous matrix of bonding material.

There are thousands of kinds of grinding wheels on the market. The abrasive grains can be larger or smaller and they can be made of harder or softer material. The various bonding materials each vitrify at different temperatures. The mix of grit to abrasive can vary, and when the materials are mixed they can be more or less compacted, affecting the amount of air in the matrix.

The color of the wheel, which can range from white to pink, blue or gray, is a clue to its composition but it doesn't reliably mean anything. Out of all the possible combinations of qualities, only a few grinding wheels are right for woodworking plane blades and chisels.

For grinding woodworking tools you need a coarse grit held in place by a soft bond. As the wheel works, the bond wears away. This exposes new and sharp grit to cut the metal. Such a wheel will remove the steel quickly, without overheating it.

A soft bond permits the abrasive particles to break away, exposing fresh, sharp grit.

Wheel surface magnified 8 times shows the individual particles of abrasive grit.

Reading the wheel

The label's fine print tells all

While there is no universal standard for identifying grinding wheels, it is possible to decode the manufacturer's specifications. The printed label glued to the center of the wheel gives the manufacturer's name, Norton for example, the maximum safe speed of the wheel in revolutions per minute, usually around 5500 RPM, and the wheel dimensions, for example, 6 x 3/4 x 1. These numbers refer to the diameter of the wheel in inches, its thickness in inches, and the size of the center hole in inches. Don't ever remove the label from a wheel.

Along with these readable specifications, you'll find a string of hieroglyphics printed on the label. Here is a typical example:

25A 120 H 8 V BE

The paper label on the grinding wheel tells its specifications and characteristics. The numerals 6x3/4x1 give the physical size of the wheel, 6 inches in diameter and 3/4 inch thick, plus the diameter of its bore, 1 inch. The next line, 25A120-H8VBE describes the abrasive material. The last line is the batch number and date of manufacture.

25A 120 H 8 V BE

25A Grit type

25A indicates grit type. "A" or "AO" means aluminum oxide, a grit well suited to woodworking tools. Aluminum oxide wheels usually are white or pink in color. "C" means carborundum, which is generally gray in color. For woodworking tools, choose aluminum oxide, not carborundum, because carborundum wheels generally have too hard a bond.

120 Grit size

120 is the grit size. Like sandpaper, the smaller the number, the coarser the grit. For grinding woodworking tools, get 80-grit or 120-grit. Fine grits grind more slowly, generating more heat. Coarse grits remove metal more quickly, generating less heat.

H Bond grade

H means the grade or hardness of the bond, from A (soft) to Z (hard). For woodworking tools, stay toward the soft end of the range, with G, H or I. The soft bond wears away easily, exposing new abrasive grit. Harder bonds don't readily wear away, which is the real cause of increased friction and therefore of increased heat and burning.

8 Structure

8 designates the ratio of grit to bond, on a scale of 0 (dense) to 12 (open). Open pores in the wheel's structure help clear the metal chips, and contribute to faster and cooler cutting. For woodworking tools, 8 is the right structure.

VBE Bond type

VBE is the bond type and modifier. The first letter, "V," means "vitrified", what you want for woodworking tools. Other bond types you may encounter are B for resinoid, R for rubber, E for shellac. The modifier BE indicates a general purpose tool-grinding bond.

Mounting the wheel

Spacer matches hole to mandrel

The wheel mounts on the grinder mandrel, with a large cupped washer on either side. Before you mount or dismount any grinding wheel, unplug the grinder motor. Do not rely on the on-off switch — it's too easy to bump it with the handle of a tool.

Always unplug the machine before working on it.

Most bench grinders have a 1/2-inch mandrel, whereas the center hole in most grinding wheels is 1 inch. If the hole in the wheel is not the same diameter as the mandrel, make it fit by inserting spacers. Wheels come with cylindrical plastic spacers like the ones shown in the photo. They're liable to drift in the hole, but you can trap them with a piece of tape. Leave the label on the wheel when you fit it on the mandrel. Add the flange-style washers that came with the grinder, and tighten the nut with a box wrench or a socket wrench. You don't have to turn the nut down hard because the direction of rotation tightens it anyway. You must not leave out the washers, nor substitute them. Use what came with the grinder and nothing else.

Plastic spacers match the hole diameter to the grinder mandrel. A loose-fitting wheel will not run true.

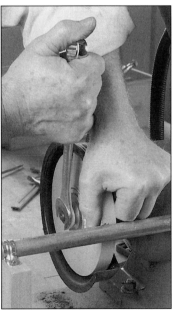

Tighten the mandrel nut with a box wrench. Make it snug.

Grinder safety

Test the wheel for cracks

A cracked wheel is extremely dangerous. The crack is hardly ever visible to the eye, but it is readily apparent to the ear. Before you mount a wheel on your grinder, check it to see whether it is sound.

Test a wheel by holding it on your finger, or on a pencil or a dowel, and give it a light tap with a hammer. A good wheel rings. A cracked wheel emits a dull thud. **You must discard a cracked wheel.** Don't run it, or you will risk the serious consequences of it flying apart.

Test the wheel by tapping it with a hammer. A good wheel rings, while a cracked one makes a dull thud. Throw cracked wheels away.

Wheel wobbles

Wheels sometimes wobble from side to side, even when correctly mounted. This wobble results from a variety of factors, including unevenness in the flanged washers, sloppiness in the spacers, and slight differences in wheel thickness. To correct the wobble, unplug the machine, loosen the nut a trifle, and rotate the wheel against the washers. Tighten the nut and test the machine. It will take a bit of fiddling, but you will be able to find the wobble-free sweet spot. And when you do, make corresponding marks on the washers and the mandrel, with an indelible marker.

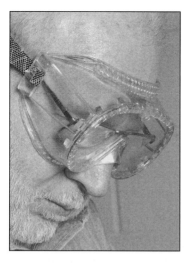

Wear your safety glasses

Shop manuals are full of safety exhortations, which people commonly ignore. But there is nothing optional or casual about wearing safety glasses when grinding.

Always wear eye protection when you grind tools. Wear plastic goggles, which can enclose regular eyeglasses, or wear safety glasses with side shields. Grinding throws off a lot of fine abrasive particles, which you absolutely do not want in your eyes.

Don't ignore this warning. Wear your safety glasses.

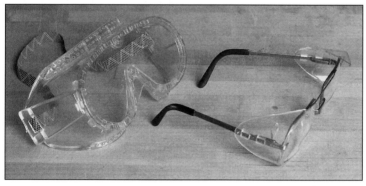

Wheel guards

Standard grinders come equipped with plastic top guards, which usually work well and should not be removed. Use the guard along with safety glasses, as exctra insurance.

Make a bottom guard to protect yourself from accidentally touching a running wheel. Grinders differ, but usually you can make a bottom guard, under the bar-style tool rest, using parts of the standard tool rest that came with the machine.

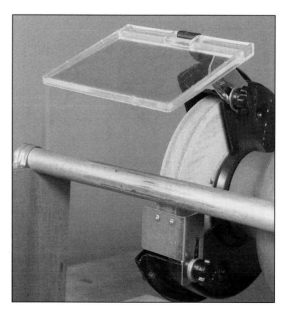

Mount the tool posts and tool rest atop the plywood grinder base. Then clamp the grinder base to the workbench.

Chapter 3

Equipping the grinder

The problem with most bench grinders is the tool rest that the manufacturer supplies. It's generally too small, too flimsy and too inaccurate. Aftermarket tool rests are all unnecessarily complicated, too small, and built around sliding parts where grit easily gets trapped between the parts, gumming up the works. The alternative is to build your own tool rest from a round steel bar, like the one shown in the photo. This is a superb solution, because it works better than any aftermarket rest I've seen, and the price can't be beat.

The tool rest is mounted on the grinder base, also shop made. Use the tool rest in conjunction with a blade holder, which you can make for chisels, plane irons and spokeshaves.

Where to put the grinder
Here are three good alternatives

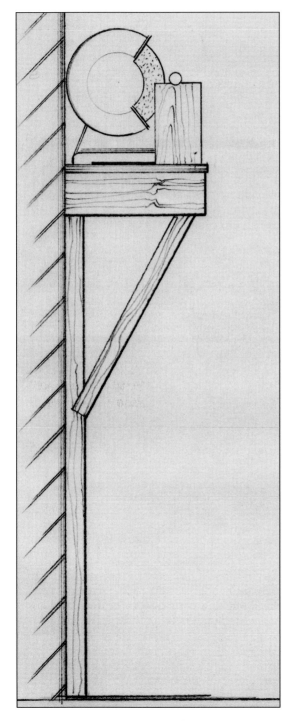

It's essential to be able to grind tools, but unless you're a woodturner it's not something you have to do every day. In fact once you've prepared your edge tools correctly, you'll be able to sharpen often but grind seldom. When it is time to grind, there'll be no big hassle, once you devise a set-up that works for you. Three good choices:

Clamp the grinder base to the bench when you need to grind tools, then unclamp it and store it away on a shelf. As a furniture maker who works alone, this is what I prefer. I don't often grind, but when I do, I like to set up and attend to all the tools that need it. Grinding makes a mess, but the loose grit is easy to vacuum up before getting back to work.

Mount the grinder base on a wall-hung shelf. Locate the grinder well away from the workbench and finishing areas of the shop, because otherwise the grit can be a nuisance.

Make a roll-away stand. In a shop where several people share common equipment, this may be the best alternative. The stand should have a low shelf with a rail all around it, to trap various tool holders and other gear. Make it so the wheels lock.

Make the grinder base plate

The grinder base plate is a rectangular piece of 3/4-inch or 1-inch hardwood plywood, measuring 9 inches by 24 inches. You can substitute medium-density fiberboard, particleboard, or 1-inch die board.

The exact location of the mounting holes depends on the configuration of your particular grinder. Once you've located them, drill and counter-bore the plywood for 3/8-inch hex-head machine bolts.

Before you drill holes for the tool rest, test the set-up with the parts you plan to use. The center of the tool rest should be at the same height as the center of the grinding wheel, with a gap of about 1/8 inch between rest and wheel. There is no need to make a science of the height - 1/2 inch up or down makes no difference.

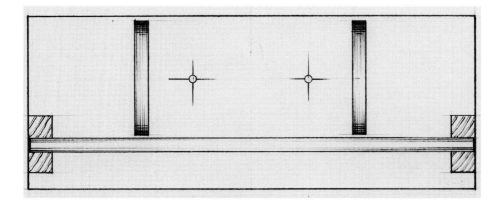

GRINDER BASE AND TOOL REST

Tool rest. 3/4 dia. mild steel rod
Base. Birch plywood. 24 x 9 x 1
Tool post. 5 x 3 x 1-1/4
Motor held to base with 2-1/4 x 3/8 flat-head machine screws.

Locate mounting holes to match grinder base.
Position the tool posts so there is 1/8-in clearance between the grinding wheel and the tool rest.

Make the tool rest posts

The two posts that support the tool rest are made from blocks of a mild hardwood, such as poplar or mahogany. Three 2-1/2 or 3 inch steel screws driven through the base and into each post will make an adequate attachment; increase the strength by angling the screws as shown. While it's not vital, there's no harm in adding a glue block.

Attach the tool rest to the posts with 1/2-inch electrical conduit straps. The straps won't fit tight unless you also make a 1/8-in. cutout in the top of each post, for the tool rest itself. Make this cutout by drilling a 3/4-inch hole in the middle of the post material, before you crosscut it to length. Position the posts so the bar is about 1/8 inch from the wheel.

TOOL REST POSTS

Saw a piece of hardwood 12 x 3 x 1-1/4.
Drill a 3/4-in. hole on center.
Crosscut the block into two posts, leaving 1/8 in. of hole in each piece.

Trim the posts to 5 in. overall length.
Screw the tool rest posts to the grinder base plate. Drive three long screws.
Fasten the tool rest to the posts with 1/2-in. electrical conduit straps.

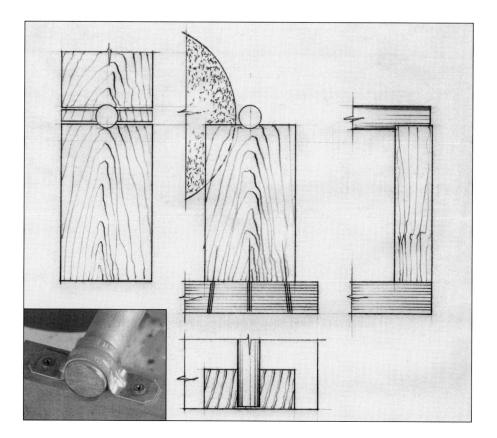

Holder for grinding plane blades
Block-and-bolt is extremely accurate

The plane-blade holder establishes the grinding angle, and ensures a square and straight edge. It consists of a hardwood block with a fence glued to one side. A bolt holds the plane blade in place. By drilling more than one bolt hole, you can use the same holder for standard-width 2 inch and 2-3/8 inch plane blades. Then make a similar but smaller holder for block-plane blades, or make a cutout for them at the other end of the regular holder, as shown in the photo below.

The grinding angle comes from how far the plane blade projects beyond the end of the holder. There is no "correct" angle for grinding plane blades. Though 25 degrees is usual, it can vary by 5 degrees either way. Consistency is more important than angular precision.

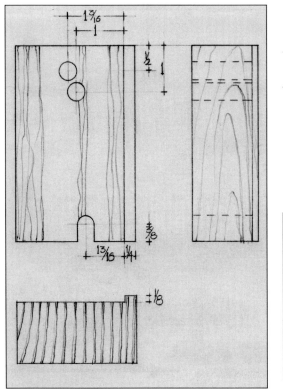

Make a block 4 in. x 2-9/16 in x 1-3/8 in.
Rebate block to create fence, or glue on a thin strip of wood.
Two drilled holes accept 2-3/8 in. and 2 in. bench plane blades.
Slot fits block plane blades.
Fasten blade with 3/8-in. bolt and wing nut or machine nut.

PLANE BLADE HOLDER

Bolt the plane blade to the holder. Make sure it's tight against the fence.

Block plane blades

The blades of block planes are smaller than regular bench plane blades, but they'll fit the regular plane blade holder. You will need to drill a new bolt hole in the other end of the holder, and since the wood is liable to break out there, elongate the hole into a slot. If you have a lot of block planes, you could also make a holder specifically for them.

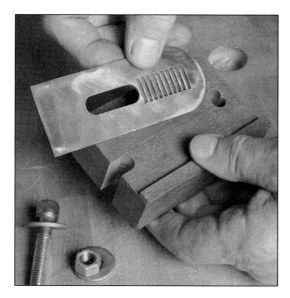

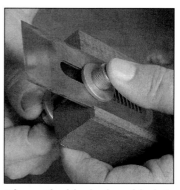

Clamp the block plane blade in the holder, using the slotted end. The bolt fits through the center of the hole in the blade. Press the blade against the fence, and check it for square.

Setting the plane blade

To calibrate the holder, snug the bolt on the plane blade and let it project about 2-1/2 inches. Set the holder on the tool rest and test-grind. You'll be able to see whether the angle is the same one you started with, or whether it is more or less. Check the newly ground metal with a protractor, and adjust the projection until the angle is what you want — extend the blade a bit more to lower the angle, and retract it a bit to increase the angle. You'll find that it's very sensitive to small adjustments, but trial and error will get the angle you want. Measure the projection and remember it, or write it on the base plate. Another way to record the setting is to butt the holder against the grinder base, mark how far the plane blade projects, and put a stop block there. This setting will be good as long as the grinding wheel remains the same diameter. As the wheel wears down, it will get smaller, and the plane blade will have to project farther.

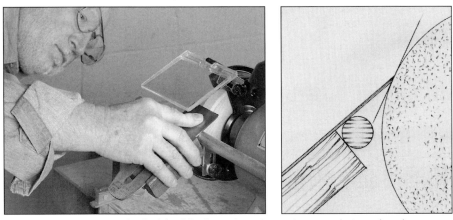

Butt the holder block against the tool rest and pivot the plane blade onto the wheel.

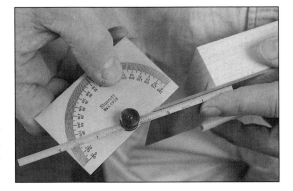

Check the grinding angle with a machinist's protractor. Here the grinding angle is exactly 25 degrees.

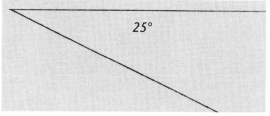

25°

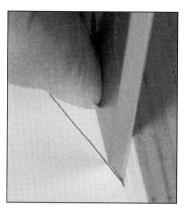

Another way to check *the grinding angle is with a drawing. Draw 25 degrees, or trace it from this page. Set the plane blade on the drawing. The blade in the photo at right is about 24 degrees, close enough.*

When the angle *is correct, butt the blade holder against the grinder base and draw the projection.*

Slide the blade *forward to the projection marked on the grinder base and tighten the bolt.*

Screw a stop block *to the line on the grinder base. Now you can set how far the blade projects from the holder by bringing the blade up to the stop block.*

Holder for grinding chisels
Shop-built dingus holds all widths

You can make a universal chisel holder out of hard wood or mild steel. The holder doesn't have to be fancy or elaborate — it just has to hold the chisel at a consistent and reproducible angle. The angle is determined by how far the chisel projects from the holder. Use a try square to set the chisel square to the edge of the holder.

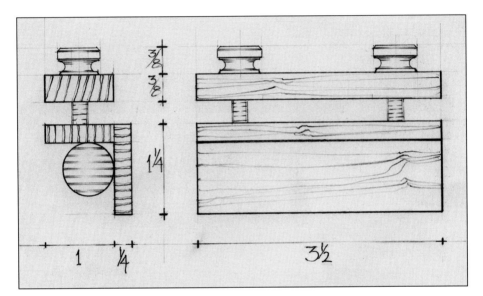

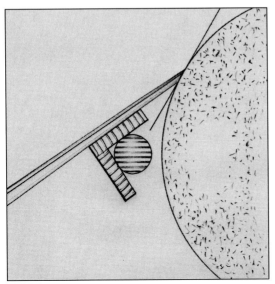

WOOD OR METAL CHISEL HOLDER

Make the chisel holder from hard wood, or from standard hardware-store iron bar and angle.

Flat-head bolts with wing nuts or knurled nuts lock the chisel in place.

Countersink the holes for flat-head bolts.

This chisel holder rides on top of the tool rest, as shown at left.

Make chisel holders from wood or from metal. These holders will accept stubby chisels, bench chisels or mortising chisels.

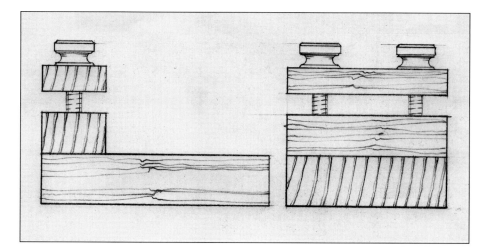

WOODEN CHISEL HOLDER

Base   *3/4 x 3-1/2 x 2-1/2*
Spacer *5/8 x 1 x 2-1/2*
Clamp *3/8 x 1 x 2-1/2*
Bolts   *1/4 x 2-1/2 flat-head*

Make spacer thick enough to clear handles of stubby chisels.
Glue spacer to base.
Clamp and drill all three pieces together.
Countersink bolt heads in base.
Clamp chisel with wing-nuts or knurled nuts.

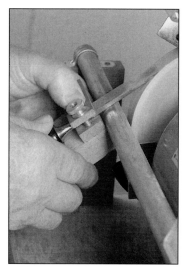

Butt the chisel holder against the tool rest and pivot the chisel onto the wheel.

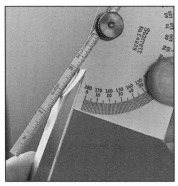

18 degrees.

Setting the chisel

There is no "correct" angle for grinding chisels. Many woodworkers use the same 25-degree angle as for plane irons, though I prefer a steeper angle of 18 degrees to 20 degrees.

To calibrate the chisel holder, let the test chisel project about 2-1/2 inches, make sure it's square, and try a test grind. Check the angle with a protractor, and adjust the projection until it is what you want. Small adjustments will make a big difference.

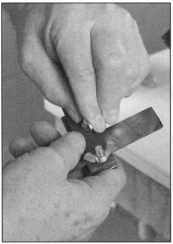

Mark various projections, which correspond to grinding angles, on the base of the grinder.

Bolt the chisel into the holder. This holder is made from angle iron.

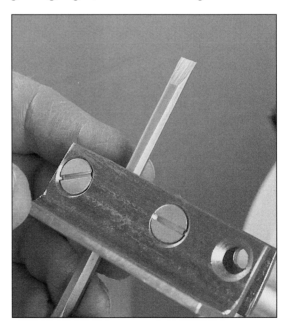

The same holder can accommodate narrow chisels as well as wide ones.

Holder for spokeshaves
Make a holder for each type of blade

Spokeshave blades typically are 2-1/8 inches wide and less than that in length. They are too small for the chisel and plane-iron holders. You can make a wooden holder for each variety of blade in your kit of tools, The principle is the same in each case: the holder runs on the tool-rest bar, it doesn't contact the grinding wheel, and it holds the blade firmly. A drawing of this holder appears on page 83.

Spokeshave blade holder is a piece of wood with a sawn slot for the blade, glued to a second block. The nut and bolt fasten the blade in the holder.

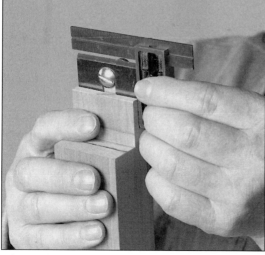

Clamp the spokeshave blade in the holder. Check it for square.

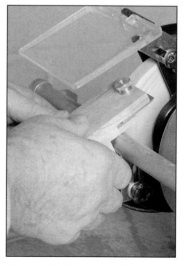

The holder's long body allows you to get a good grip and to maintain the grinding angle.

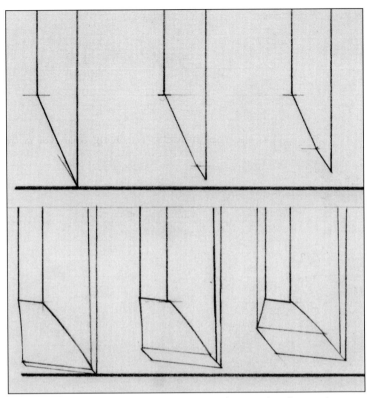

Every time you sharpen, the blade gets shorter, the sharpening bevel gets bigger, and sharpening takes longer. When it takes too long, it's time to regrind.

CHAPTER 4

When to grind

Regrind a tool whenever sharpening takes too long. Extra time sharpening indicates that repeated trips to the waterstones have widened the sharpening bevel, increasing the amount of metal that has to be removed. Grinding reshapes the sharpening bevel by making it narrow again.

Grind also when the cutting edge is out of square, when you want to change the angle of the bevel to suit a difficult wood, or when the edge has been nicked.

Grinding is an abrasive process, which produces heat. The whole trick is to avoid generating so much heat that you burn the steel or draw its temper. This is why to use a soft, slow-running wheel, and keep the tool moving over the surface of the wheel with a light touch that gets lighter as the bevel gets nearer to a feather edge.

Practice to acquire skill

To begin, wear eye protection and wear an apron. Stand in front of the grinder, don't sit, because good technique requires moving freely. With the grinder motor switched off, mount the tool in its holder and get the feel of moving it from side to side on the tool rest. Improve the action by rubbing paraffin wax onto the contact areas of the tool rest and on the tool holders. The long tool rest is designed to give you room to work, and allows you to slide the tool beyond the wheel to the right or to the left.

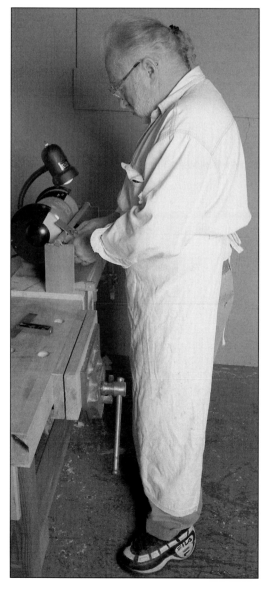

Even with a good tool rest and a suitable holder, grinding is a hand process that puts the tool at risk and requires skill. You'll acquire the feel of it by practicing — the more you grind, the better you'll get. This is another reason why it makes sense to pile up tool grinding and do it all at once. To do it well you have to get into it and spend some time. You'll be rewarded by the improvement in your tools, and in your skills at the workbench.

Grinding stance. Stand comfortably at the grinder, so you can move sideways from the feet and legs. Wear safety glasses and an apron.

Grinding plane blades

Mount the plane blade in its holder and adjust how far it projects to get the angle you want. (page 30).

Start the motor and plant the blade holder on the tool rest, with its back end low so the bevel doesn't contact the wheel. Use your right hand to keep the tool holder in contact with the rest, and use your left hand to move the holder from side to side.

Now pivot the tool into contact with the grinding wheel. Don't press hard, but do pay attention to the feel of steel on the wheel. Slowly move the tool from side to side, maintaining light and even pressure. Change direction when the edge of the plane iron just passes the edge of the wheel, as

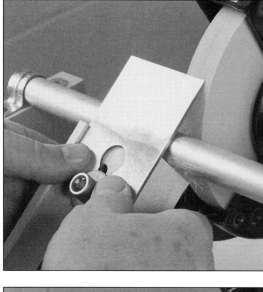

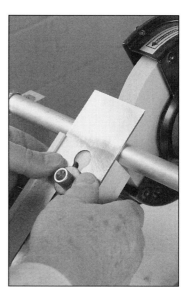

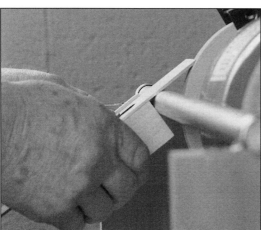

Press the tool holder against the rest and traverse from side to side. Change direction when the corner of the blade just passes the edge of the wheel. To apply light pressure, grip the tool holder gently and loosely.

The amount of blade projecting from the tool holder determines the grinding bevel.

shown in the photos. If you go too far, so that only a small portion of the blade remains on the wheel, you'll probably burn the steel.

Heat comes from friction; press harder, more heat. As the grinding bevel gets bigger, decrease the pressure. The grinding bevel does not extend all the way to the edge of the tool. Ease up and leave a tiny bit of the original sharpened edge.

Grinding the bevel until it meets the back face creates a feather edge at the very tip of the tool. You have to be extremely careful to avoid burning the steel, because there's not enough mass to dissipate the heat. There's no need to grind a feather edge, because woodworking tools always have a second, sharpening bevel that is created and maintained on flat waterstones.

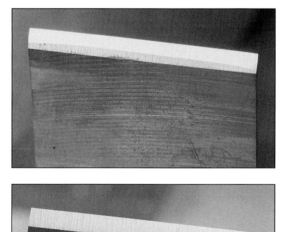

Blunt. This plane blade is ready to re-grind, because a half-dozen trips to the waterstone have enlarged the sharpening bevel. There is more metal to remove each time, so sharpening takes longer.

Ground. Several passes across the grinding wheel have reduced the sharpening bevel to a thin line. The iron is ready to sharpen.

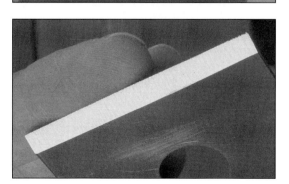

Feather edge. Grinding until the bevel meets the back face produces a feather edge. Avoid creating a feather edge because it is too thin to shed the heat.

Grinding bench chisels

Chisels are different from plane irons because most of them are narrower than the wheel itself. Also, the blades aren't always strictly rectangular in section, so they don't sit well in the holder. Therefore, whenever you mount the chisel in the grinding holder, check that it is sitting straight and square.

Establish the grinding angle by calibrating a test chisel and then record the distance it protrudes from the holder, as discussed on page 34. I prefer a lower angle than the standard 25 degrees, somewhere between 18 degrees and 20 degrees. The long bevel not only looks elegantly sharp, it improves visibility in tight spots, such as when paring dovetails.

When the chisel is narrower than the grinding wheel, instead of traversing the wheel with the tool, pivot the tool holder to dab the metal gently onto the stone. Control the dabbing motion and the pressure with one hand, and the side-to-side motion with the other. A light touch is all it takes, and the narrower the chisel, the gentler the action.

A long bevel, this one is 18 degrees, works well on bench chisels.

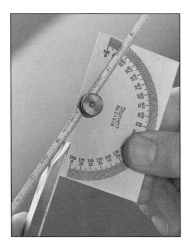

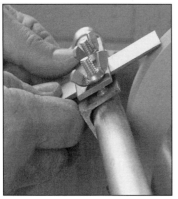

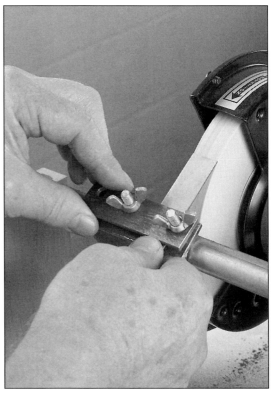

Pivot the tool holder against the tool rest with one hand, and slide it from side to side with the other hand.

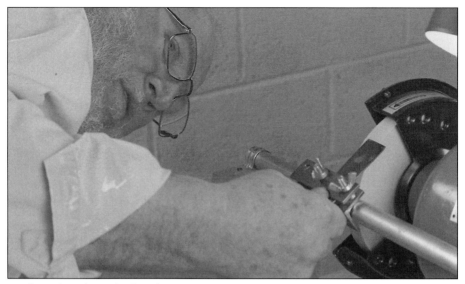

Look and see *how the bevel contacts the grinding wheel. To change the bevel, adjust the projection from the holder.*

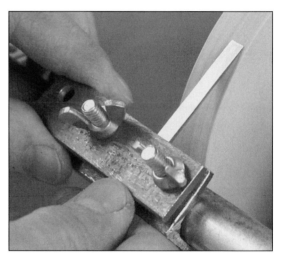

When grinding *narrow chisels, minimize the buildup of heat by dabbing the the chisel onto the wheel.*

Mortise chisels

Mortise chisels are ground at 25 degrees. Grinding on a wheel makes a hollow shape, which isn't as strong as a flat grind. However, the 25-degree hollow grind is workable and strong enough. The alternative is to grind the chisel on the flat side of the wheel, which is not safe because the wheel is not designed to resist sideways pressure. Don't try to grind the mortise chisel to a sharper angle than 25 degrees. It would be too fragile.

Cooling the steel

Burned steel will not hold an edge.

Some grinders have a water trough cast into the base. Elsewhere you find a coffee-can of water next to the grinder. You could be forgiven for thinking that an overheated blade could be plunged into the cool water and saved. Not so.

It usually goes like this: you grind the blade and you hope you won't overheat it. Suddenly you see oxidation colors appear on the metal, moving quickly from straw through blue to purple, ending in barbecue black. You quickly quench the steel in water. However, by the time you see the colors, it is too late — the molecular change in the steel has occurred and it no longer has the ability to hold an edge. You can't slow down or reverse this change. That's not what the cooling water is for.

The purpose of the water is to cool the steel to room temperature before it loses its temper. Leaving the metal to cool in the air would also work, it just would take longer. If you add ice to the water, you can start with metal cooled to below room temperature, giving you that much more time on the grinding wheel.

How can you tell when the metal is too hot? Test it by tapping it with your fingertip. If you don't feel the heat, lay the blade on the palm of your hand. You'll know if it is too hot.

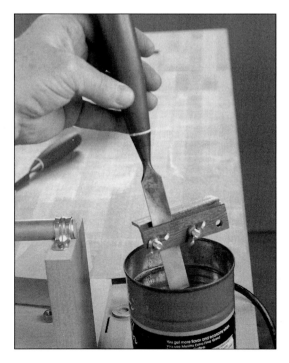

Less heat is always better, so take it easy as you grind, and pause to cool the blade before it gets too hot.

In practice, I rarely cool the blade with water. The combination of a slow and soft wheel doesn't generate enough heat to cause trouble, provided you work gently and don't push it.

Use the cooling water to bring the steel from hot-to-the-touch down to room temperature.

Truing the wheel

The grinding wheel may wear out of round, and the working face may no longer be flat or square to the sides. Hard wheels are prone to clog and glaze over, though this rarely a problem with a soft aluminum oxide wheel.

All these conditions can be put right by dressing the wheel. There are three styles of dresser in common use: a metal "star" dresser, which looks like a toothed wheel in a metal handle; a diamond dresser, which looks like a crayon; and a carborundum or Crylon dresser, which is a square stick. I prefer the carborundum dresser because it is the simplest and cheapest, so that's what's shown here.

Clamp the wheel dresser in the chisel holder and make several light passes across the face of the wheel. Take it easy, because you can destroy a wheel in no time. Shut off the wheel to check the face for squareness. Don't try to hand-hold a diamond or carborundum dresser — you don't have enough control, so it can't get the wheel true.

Controlling the mess

Whether grinding or being dressed, soft wheels throw off a lot of abrasive grit. The grit is invasive, dirty and generally nasty. Sweep it up or vacuum it up as soon as you finish grinding.

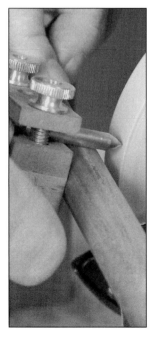

Dress the wheel with a square stick of carborundum or a diamond dresser. Clamp the dresser in the chisel holder.

Use a try square to make sure the face of the wheel is square to the sides. Stop the motor and pull the plug before making this check .

Resurrecting a damaged edge

This much-abused chisel not only suffers from an out of square edge, it's been nicked by a colliding with a nail.

Many's the mishap that can befall a woodworking chisel or plane blade. Even if you would never use it for opening paint cans, you might drop it on concrete, or drive it into a hard knot, or into metal hardware. Zealous grinding can draw the temper from the edge, burning the steel. Chisels and plane blades easily can be sharpened askew, so the edge drifts out of square with the blade. **From the repair point of view, an out-of-square edge, a nicked edge and a burned edge all require the same treatment.**

The first step is to grind the blade back beyond the damage by pushing the blade straight into the grinding wheel. There's no point in attempting to maintain the bevel during this maneuver. You'll only increase the risk of overheating the steel. Instead, grind straight across by pushing the chisel straight into the wheel. Continue to grind until no trace of the damage remains.

When restoring a burned edge, it's not enough to grind the colors off the surface of the metal. The affected metal must all be removed.

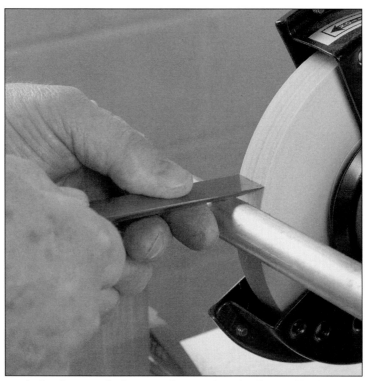

Push the damaged edge *straight into the wheel. Grind back square to clean, undamaged metal.*

Once you have cut back to a square end in undamaged steel, you can shape the grinding bevel and sharpen the edge in the usual way.

The technique of pushing the blade straight into the wheel shocks people when they see it for the first time. They want to remove the defect at the regular grinding angle. This has two problems: you have to grind to a feather edge, which increases the risk of burning the metal, and you can't see where you are going. Pushing the blade straight into the wheel and making the edge square removes the defect immediately, and it establishes the location of the new grind. It looks frightening at first, but it's the best method.

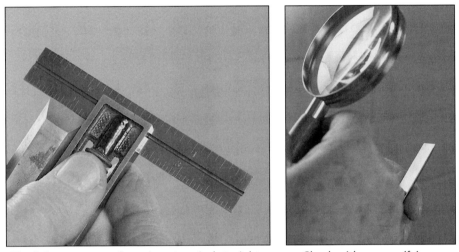

Check for square and continue to grind straight across. Check with a magnifying glass to be sure all traces of damage have been removed.

Fit the chisel into its holder and restore the grinding bevel.

New waterstones. *The three stones at top are a Japanese 1200-grit red stone, an 800-grit stone, and a 6000-grit silver stone. The two waterstones on the right are American-made equivalents. The double-sided stone in the foreground combines a coarse and medium grits.*

CHAPTER 5

Waterstones

A waterstone, which looks like a smooth clay brick, is a soft, fast-cutting abrasive lubricated with water. Normally the stone is stored ready for use in a bucket of water, which saturates its pores. To use the stone, you take it out of the bucket and mount it on a stand. As the blade squeegees the surface you keep it wet by squirting with water. The water floats the spent abrasive and metal swarf out of the way of the sharpening action.

Waterstones, like most oilstones and other sharpening products on the market today, are man-made. While natural sharpening stones still can be found, they are liable to be inconsistent in quality, or else frighteningly expensive. This is because the natural sources of good stones have been all but quarried out. Man-made stones generally are high in quality and consistent in manufacture, and their composition has been engineered for the task at hand.

Waterstones are not a new product, but since about 1980 they have become increasingly popular among woodworkers. The reasons for their popularity are not hard to find: waterstones work faster, and produce a keener edge, than other sharpening products. They come in a wide range of grades from coarse to extremely fine, they are easy to maintain, and they are relatively inexpensive.

How waterstones work

The abrasive breaks down and floats away

All man-made sharpening stones consist of a porous mix of abrasive particles set in a bonding material. As the tool is rubbed across the flat surface of the stone, the sharp abrasive grit cuts away the metal, making it smooth and flat. Working from a relatively coarse stone through a succession of fine stones puts a high polish on the metal.

The act of sharpening not only wears away the blade, it also takes the edge off the abrasive particles in the stone. More importantly, the bonding material also breaks down, exposing new and sharp abrasive particles. This is why a stone with a soft bond cuts more quickly than a hard one: the soft bonding material breaks down more easily, exposing fresh abrasive.

For the stone to be effective it is necessary to get rid of the worn abrasive particles and abraded bits of metal, or swarf. If this waste isn't removed, it will embed in the surface of the stone and glaze over, effectively stopping the cutting action. A flood of water does a better job of keeping the stone clean, than other lubricants.

When the stone has been stored under water and is totally soaked, the sharpening action produces a wet slurry of bond material and abrasive particles. This slurry isn't a problem, in fact it can help the sharpening action, but once it goes dry as the water is squeezed out it becomes difficult to continue moving the blade. A fresh squirt of water allows the stone to continue the sharpening action and prevents the dry mix from grinding into the surface.

What stones to buy?

The speed and efficiency with which a stone will sharpen a tool depends on the type and fineness of the abrasive grit, the hardness of the bonding material, and the proportion of grit to bond. As in all things, what you buy depends on your wallet's fatness, but for general sharpening you will need three stones.

Coarse stone, on which to flatten the backs of new blades.
Medium stone, to sharpen the edge of a dull blade and refine the back.
Fine stone, to refine and polish the sharpened edge and the back.

"Coarse," "medium" and "fine" are comparative terms and in fact all these stones are extremely fine when judged against what our ancestors had to work with. The 1000-grit waterstone, which the Japanese call a red stone, corresponds to a soft white Arkansas oilstone. The 4000-grit fine stone corresponds to a hard black Arkansas oilstone. The 6000-grit S1 or silver stone, and the 8000-grit G1 or gold stone, have no equivalent among natural stones.

Always buy the largest stone you can afford; the minimum is one measuring 2 1/2 in. wide by 8 in. Expect to pay between $30 and $50 for each waterstone.

Coarse — up to 800 grit — flattening stone

This stone is for the initial flattening of the backs of new tools. Once you have prepared a new tool by flattening its back, you won't need to visit the coarse stone again. It's not part of the everyday sharpening routine. Because this isn't an everyday stone, a two-sided stone is a good buy. I prefer a 100/220 grit combination.

The problem now is that our sharpening stone is 1200 grit and that's a big jump from the 220 grit. So, if you can afford it, buy a fourth stone at 600 or 800 grit. It's a luxury, but one you'll appreciate when you're conditioning new tools or restoring a batch of used ones.

Medium — 800 to 1200 grit — sharpening stone

You have three choices: 800 grit, 1000 grit, or1200 grit. This is the stone you'll use to sharpen a blade when it's blunt. As you use the blade, the wood tissue pounds and erodes the metal, tearing off microscopic particles and finally making the edge too thick to cut any more. Sharpening on the medium stone means quickly cutting the rounded edge of the sharpening bevel back to a flat face.

If you choose an 800-grit stone for sharpening, you'll cut the metal quite quickly, but you'll also leave relatively large scratches. This means correspondingly more time on the fine stone.

On the other hand, if you use 1200-grit as your sharpening stone, you'll cut the blunted bevel back more slowly, but you will leave finer grooves in the metal, and you'll spend less time polishing on the fine stone.

Since the fine stone is both more expensive and more liable to be gouged, the less time you spend on it the longer it will last. And since, the total time is the same either way, on balance you're better off with a 1200-grit sharpening stone.

Fine — 4000 to 8000 grit — polishing stone

Catalogs refer to fine stones as finishing stones, and that's what they do: refine and polish an edge that's already been shaped. I prefer the 6000-grit silver stone. It's fast cutting and quite fine enough for hand tools. The 8000-grit gold stone is expensive, finer than you need, and more trouble than you want since it's quite easy to gouge the surface.

The medium stone establishes the new edge by quickly cutting the blunt sharpening bevel back to a sharp intersection with the back of the blade. The fine stone refines the new sharpening bevel to a high polish.

WATERSTONE GRITS

Coarse	*up to 800 grit*	*Flattening back face*
Medium	*800-1000-1200*	*Sharpening*
Fine	*4000-6000, S1, G1*	*Polishing*

Keep them under water

Waterstones are porous and they need to be soaked in water for about one-half hour before use. They should be saturated and used dripping wet. It's best to store stones immersed in water. While it does not harm a stone to dry out, it does take time to get it thoroughly soaked again.

Store your stones standing upright in a bucket of water. Have a care when you drop the stones into the bucket. Try not to let them crash into one another because bits will break off. It's no problem if the stone protrudes above the surface, because capillary action will keep the whole mass saturated. If the atmosphere is dry, put a lid on the bucket and keep it topped up. If the nighttime shop temperature falls below freezing, however, bring the bucket of stones into warmer surroundings. Freezing will harm your stones by cracking or spalling their surfaces.

Under water. Store sharpening stones in a bucket of water. Keep the water topped up, and prevent it from freezing.

Flattening waterstones

Sharpening on the waterstone naturally wears it away, so it's not long before there's a hollow in the center. However, making a straight and sharp edge on a plane iron or chisel requires a flat stone. Consequently, the waterstone has to be made flat, and it will require flattening throughout its life.

To assess the condition of your waterstone, dry the surface with a paper towel and use a straightedge to gauge the wear. A dip of 1/16 inch is too great, time to flatten.

If you have gouged the surface of the stone, and you will surely know when you do, it's worth flattening it out. Gouges are annoying, but nevertheless they serve an instructive purpose, since after flattening you'll want to avoid doing it again.

Flattening the stone is reasonably quick and easy. The method is to rub the stone on a piece of wet-dry silicon-carbide abrasive paper atop a flat sheet of plate glass. Flattening can be done wet or dry, according to whether the stone in question has been stored in water, or has been allowed to dry out.

Match the wet-dry paper to the stone being flattened, as follows:

coarse stones, 120-grit wet-dry paper
medium (800-1200 grit) stones, 220-grit wet-dry paper
fine (4000-6000-grit) stones, 320- or 400-grit wet-dry paper.

FLATTENING EQUIPMENT

12-in. x 12-in. square of 1/4-in. or 3/8-in. plate glass
Plywood to support glass
Silicon carbide wet-dry sandpaper: 120-grit, 220-grit, 320-grit, 400-grit
Squeeze bottle for water

Wet-flattening

If the stone is already wet, flatten with lots of water. Soak the wet-dry paper in water and stick it to the plate glass with a squirt of water. Keep the surface flooded and add water whenever a paste or slurry begins to form. Squirt the paper to wash the slurry away.

Rub the stone in a circular or reciprocal movement, and try to maintain uniform pressure. Pause to check the stone against a steel straight-edge, then flip it end for end when you resume flattening.

Wet-flattening is a messy process, one reason why it's best to build a sharpening station as discussed on page 56. Wash the slurry into your waterstone bucket. Let any oversplash dry on the sharpening station or shop floor, then vacuum up the dried powder.

The same paper can be re-used two or three times, provided you let it dry out in between. It will curl up but will be fine when it's re-soaked. Don't leave the paper in water, because the abrasive will fall off within a day or two.

Wet flattening. Squirt plenty of water on the stone and sandpaper. The dark place in the center of the stone is a hollow caused by use.

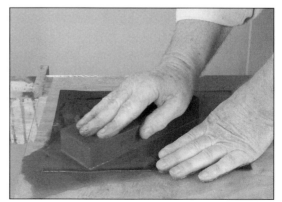

Work the stone back and forth on the abrasive.

Dry-flattening

If the stone is dry, flatten it dry. It's quicker than wet-flattening and not nearly as messy. Dry-flatten by putting the paper on a piece of plate glass. Dry-flattening will fill up the wet-dry paper with fine dust. If you brush it clean and vacuum up the dust, it should last for many flattenings.

Since dry-flattening is so much quicker and cleaner, you may find it worthwhile to invest in a second set of stones. Keep one set soaking in the bucket, ready to sharpen tools. Let the other set dry out for flattening.

Dry flattening. If the stone is dry, flattening without water avoids a mess.

When to stop

Once you begin the flattening process, it's very easy to check your progress: just look at the stone. The newly flattened portion of its surface will appear clean and uniform in color. Hollow places will appear dark and untouched by the abrasive paper. When the full surface of the stone looks clean and smooth, it's probably flat enough. However, make a final check with the steel straight-edge.

Small nicks don't matter. Flattening fills small nicks with abrasive powder, which contrasts with the surface of the stone. Small nicks won't affect sharpening.

It's flat. When the surface of the stone looks uniform and smooth, it's probably flat. Check it with a steel straight-edge.

Alternatives to waterstones

While waterstones produce the best edge in the least amount of time, if you already own oilstones, diamond stones or ceramic sharpening plates, there's no need to discard your investment and start over. You can create an edge with most of the other sharpening systems on the marketplace. In a time of no money, you can even put an edge on tools with wet-dry sandpaper on a piece of plate glass. The big problem with all other stones is the final refining or polish of the newly sharpened edge. Oilstones and diamond-impregnated plates do an acceptable job of resharpening, but they can't polish as smoothly as the fine S1 waterstone.

Oilstones

Manufactured carborundum and India oilstones are consistent in quality. They are both good for removing metal, so long as they are not clogged with dust or glazed with chips. Compared to waterstones, they are slow to wear hollow, but they are much more difficult to flatten. Instead of wet-dry paper, you have to use carborundum powders on plate glass. Natural Arkansas oilstones are quite inconsistent. Natural stones often contain anomalies, which are liable to leave an abrasive scar on the tool. As suitable material becomes more difficult to find and quarry, stones large enough for woodworking tools become prohibitively expensive.

Carborundum oilstones *often come with coarse grit on one side and medium on the other.*

Stone manufacturers sell expensive little bottles of special honing oil. You don't have to pay the high price. What's needed is a light, watery oil that can float the swarf away from the action. A 50-50 mixture of ordinary lubricating oil in kerosene works fine. A mixture of 75% kerosene with 25% motor oil also works.

Oilstones are prone to clogging in the dust of the workshop. Keep them covered.

Diamond-impregnated plates

Diamond-impregnated plates consist of a metal plate, usually of stainless steel, with industrial diamond dust sintered onto its surface. Since they are a manufactured product, the diamond grits are generally uniform and consistent. They are also expensive.

Unlike other materials, diamond abrasive stays sharp because of diamond's incredible hardness and wear resistance. The surface of the plate doesn't break down to expose new cutting surfaces. This means that once the diamond plate does become clogged or dull, there's not much you can do to renew it.

Diamond plates remove metal quickly. They can be used with water or oil. A coarse diamond plate is a good alternative to the coarse waterstone, though it may cost four times as much.

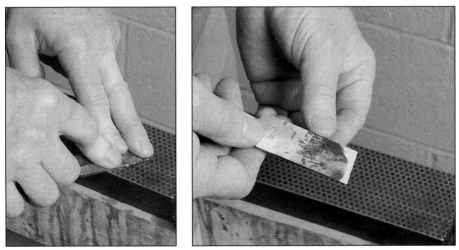

Diamond-impregnated plates make short work of flattening the back face of chisels and plane blades.

Shop-built sharpening station holds sharpening stones, flattening plate, and water bucket. Tailor it to your own height.

CHAPTER 6

Sharpening station

The main reason people have trouble sharpening is, they try to work at the wrong height. You need to get your body above the waterstone and hold the tool at arm's length. The motion comes from the shoulders, not from the wrists.

For this reason you cannot sharpen on a regular workbench. It's too high. It's also a messy process, and the gritty water will destroy the workbench.

The net result is that you need to build a dedicated sharpening station. It is a small, low stand designed for waterstones,

flattening plate, and water bucket. The top is open so water can drip through. You can make any of three types of stand:

> a free-standing piece of shop furniture,
> an outrigger that can be attached to the workbench,
> a wall-hung structure.

My choice is the free-standing version, which is detailed on the following pages. It doesn't take a lot of room, and it's light and easy to move. Because it's the right height for sharpening, the sharpening station is the wrong height for everything else, so it's always ready when you need it.

Tailor the station to your height

To build the sharpening station, the critical dimension is its height, which equals the length of the leg pieces. The correct height turns out to be the distance from your fingertips to the ground when you stand naturally and relaxed, minus the thickness of your waterstones. If there's any uncertainty in the measurement, go for lower instead of higher.

An outrigger sharpening station can hook onto the end of the workbench. The same design can also be attached to the wall. There's a construction drawing on page 63.

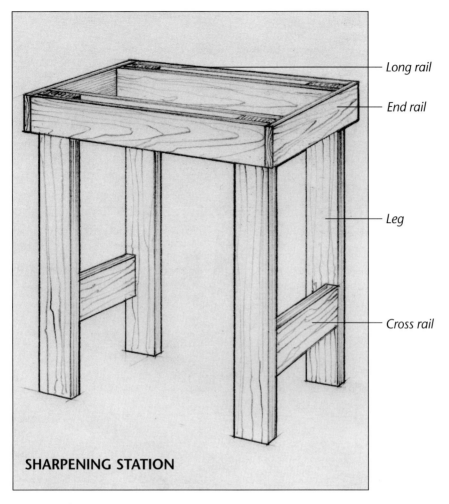

SHARPENING STATION

CUTTING LIST

Part	Qty	Dimension	Notes
Leg	4	1-1/2 x 3-1/2 x 27	2x4
Long rail	4	3/4 x 3-1/2 x 23	1x4
End rail	2	3/4 x 3-1/2 x 17	1x4
Cross rail	2	1 1/2 x 3-1/2 x 13	Trim to fit

SHOPPING LIST

12 feet of 2x4
12 feet of 1x4
1-1/4-inch and 2-inch galvanized screws

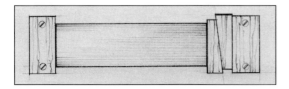

Detail of stop block and stone-retaining wedges.

Sharpening station

The goal of this project is a sturdy little stand that won't flex or bounce around, and that will last for years. It's made out of stock 2x4s, though it will help to select clear and straight-grained wood. These instructions go into detail for what is, after all, a simple project. If you're an experienced woodworker, you can ignore the instructions and build it any way you like. But if you are a beginning woodworker, you'll find a quick and practical general-purpose building method in these instructions.

Building the sharpening station

1. Saw the wood. Cut all the parts to length at one time. Square crosscuts are important, so make some test cuts and check them for square before you start.

2. Set up the first joint. The first joint, between a long rail and a leg, establishes the pattern of work for the project. In this case, all the joints will be glued and secured with #6 x 2-inch galvanized screws, four per joint. Set the rail on the leg with an offset of 1/8 inch, as shown in the illustration, with a scrap of 2x4 supporting the free end of the leg. Check it for square and draw a layout line where the parts fit together.

2. Set up the first joint and make it square.

3. Spread the glue. Take the pieces apart, and roll glue inside the layout lines. A small, disposable paint roller is the easiest way to spread and manage woodworking glue. When it's not in use, keep the roller wet with glue, in its tray, inside a zipped-up freezer bag. It will keep that way for many months, same as it does inside the bottle.

4. Screw the rail to the leg. Reassemble the rail and leg, check for square again, and if the glue floats around, clamp the piece to the worktable. Drill four pilot holes through the rail into the leg, and countersink for the screw heads. Drive four of the 2-inch screws into the joint. Drive the screws down firm and tight, so their heads bite into the wood.

3. Spread the glue inside the layout lines on the rail and leg.

4. Screw the rail to the leg.

5. Screw the rail to the second leg. Glue and screw another leg to the free end of the long rail. Then glue and screw the other two legs to the other long rail. This makes two U-shaped leg-and-rails frames.

6. Add the second set of rails. There's a second long rail connecting each pair of legs. The pairs of long rails not only make the sharpening station incredibly strong, they also form its working surfaces. Glue and screw these long rails to the legs.

7. Join the two frames. The end rails join the two halves of the station together. Stand the pieces on end on the worktable, as shown in the photo, and glue and screw the first end rail to the ends of the long rails. Drive four #6 x 2-1/2 galvanized screws into each joint. Turn the assembly over and join the other end rail in the same way.

5. Screw the rail to the second leg.

6. Add the second set of rails.

7. Join the two frames.

8. Add the cross rails. Construction 2x4s are liable to twist and bend, so add two cross rails between the faces of the legs. Measure the distance between the legs at the top of the stand, and cut the cross rails to that length. Lay the sharpening station on its side on the worktable. Then tap each cross rail into position near the bottom of the legs. Check for square. Drill pilot holes and screw through the face of the legs into the end-grain of the cross rails with 3-inch #8 screws.

9. Fit the stop blocks. The stop blocks keep the waterstones from sliding off the sharpening station. They're tapered so they can wedge tightly together. Fit the stop blocks to your stones and screw them to the rails.

9. Fit the stop blocks.

8. Add the cross rails.

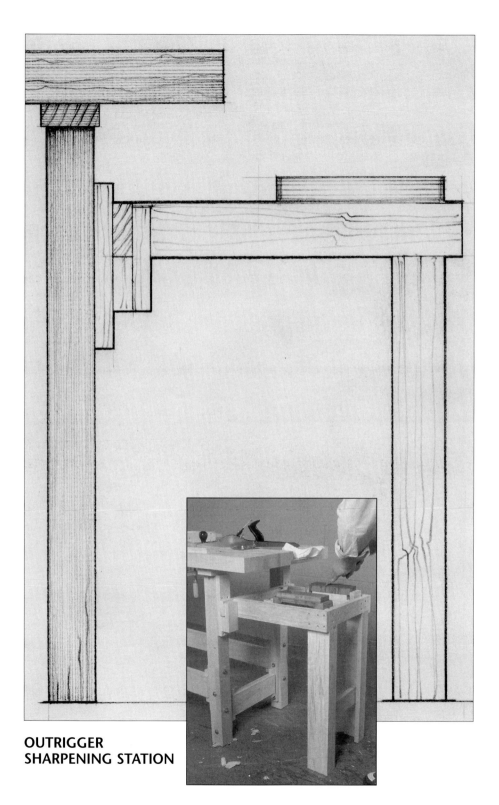

**OUTRIGGER
SHARPENING STATION**

The back face of a new tool may look flat and smooth, but it's not. It has to be flattened and polished.

CHAPTER 7

The back face

Chisels and plane blades have two deficiencies as they come from the manufacturer.

The back face is not flat.
Its surface is not smooth.

The degree of flatness may be quite bad and obviously so, or it may be OK. It's the luck of the draw, but in any case check the back face with a steel straight edge.

Surface roughness is visible to the naked eye, but for a new perspective take a look through a hand lens. Hollows, bumps and scratches will show up as dull places and nicks in the cutting edge.

Sharpening a blade with score marks on its back face is like trying to make a scalpel out of a steak knife. No matter how much you work on the sharpening bevel, the serrations don't go away, and they will show up as raised lines on your work.

Every new tool must be flattened on its back face, before it can be sharpened and put to work. This is because the intersection of the sharpening bevel and the back face is what forms the sharp edge. Both surfaces must be free of machine marks or grinding marks, or else the edge will be nicked. The goal is:

Flat.
Mirror-smooth.

Flatten when the tool is new

Flattening only has to be done once in the life of a blade. Get it right, and it stays right.
Every time you sharpen the blade, you will visit its back face with the fine waterstone. This step removes the burr and improves smoothness right up to the cutting edge. This is called "backing off" (page 81).
You can't tell how much metal has to be removed to flatten the back face until you begin the process. Begin on your coarse waterstone. Once you've removed the deep scratches and valleys, the tool will be ready to move to the medium stone and finally to the fine stone, where the steel acquires its mirror finish.
If you purchase used woodworking tools, don't expect them to be flat. The truth is that they never did "make them like they used to." You'll get best results if you treat the used tool as if it was new, and go through the whole process of preparing it for first use.
A flat waterstone is essential for flattening the back face. If there's any doubt about the condition of the stone, prepare it as discussed on page 51.

The dark areas show where the stone has removed metal. The light areas are hollows that have not yet come in contact with the stone.

How to flatten the back face

Having soaked the coarse waterstone, flood it with water and lay the blade across its full width, as much of the blade as will fit. Now work the blade from one end of the stone to the other, exerting as much downward pressure as you can. The metal area is large, so it takes a lot of work to flatten it. On the coarse side of a 100/250 combination stone, you might have to work on it for 10 or 20 minutes, or even longer. You'll quickly see why the stone has to be low enough to get your upper body right on top of the action.

Pause and check the back face of the blade. You'll see where the stone has begun to cut the high spots, and the low spots where it hasn't yet touched the metal.

The objective is to level out all the high spots, so the scratch pattern left by the coarse stone extends fully across the blade's back face, and right to the cutting edge. It might take only a few minutes, but it might take a half-hour of hard work.

What you now have is a flat back that is covered with grooves caused by the coarse stone. The next step is to retain the flatness while refining the grooved surface. Move to a stone that is less coarse — if you're using a combination stone, flip it over to the 250-grit side. Get right on top of the work and press hard, as with the coarse stone. Work the blade from one end of the stone to the other.

Lay the blade's back face across the coarse waterstone. Press hard, and work from one end of the stone to the other.

The scratch pattern shows that the coarse stone has removed metal all across the back face.

Some new blades are so badly distorted that it doesn't seem possible ever to flatten the whole of the back face. When you find yourself in that situation, with stiff fingers and sore shoulders, it's only sensible to retreat. Concentrate the pressure on the half-inch of steel leading up to the very edge, and leave the remainder of the back for another day.

Once the stone has made the surface look the same uniform grey, it's time to refine these scratches on the medium waterstone. You will see a dramatic difference when you finally get to the fine stone, because it's here that your earlier haste to get on with it shows up – as marks which the fine stone will take forever to remove. You have to decide whether to go back to a coarser stone to remove these fissures, or to live with the results in hand.

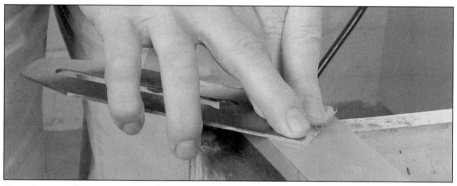

Continue to flatten on a medium waterstone. Press hard at the edge of the blade.

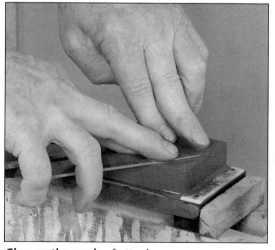

Change the angle of attack as you progress to finer stones, so the blade comes close to being in line with the stone's long edge.

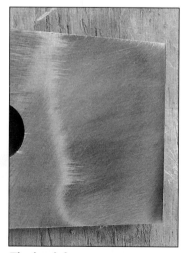

The back face comes up to a uniform shine. This blade is ready to sharpen.

Checking for flatness

Check the blade with a straight edge. The severest test of flatness is to hold the blade like a mirror and capture the reflection of a fluorescent tube. If the tube appears perfectly straight, the surface is flat. If it bends, a hill or a hollow remains in the metal, or perhaps you have succeeded in rounding over the end.

Checking for smooth

You can't easily tell when it's time to move to a finer stone, though a hand magnifier helps a lot. Move on when you think the blade is ready, but pause after a minute to look at the back face again. If the blade still has hills and hollows, they'll be clearly visible now, and you'll probably have to go back to the coarse stone to remove them. In the end you will begin to see your own reflection — the better it gets, the smoother the surface.

Fettling the plane's cap iron

"Fettling" is an old word that means "preparing for use," as in the expression, "He's in fine fettle." Flattening the back of a new blade is part of the process of fettling. But with planes there's more.

Bench planes have a cap iron that fits tightly on the blade. Its leading edge presses on the back face of the blade about

Before you disassemble the cap iron from the blade, take a close look at how they fit together.

1/16 inch from the edge. The cap iron turns the shaving, causing it to curl, and it also supports the blade, suppressing vibration. In order to work, the cap iron and blade have to be in tight contact across their full width. Before you disassemble the cap iron from the blade, take a close look through a hand lens at the line of contact. Note where it fits and where it doesn't.

Now separate the parts and lay the cap iron onto the 1200-grit medium sharpening stone. Raise the back end of the cap iron to clear the stone by a whisker, so only the front edge makes contact, and work it flat and smooth. Touch up on the fine stone, then dub off the sharp edge.

Fettling a chisel

Fettling also improves a new chisel. The long corner between the back face and the edges usually is sharp enough to fillet your index finger. Put the corner on the 1200-grit stone at a 45-degree angle. Take four to six strokes to remove the sharp edge and any burr associated with it. This makes the chisel friendly to your fingers, ready to work for you.

Lay the cap iron flat on the medium waterstone to straighten and polish its working edge.

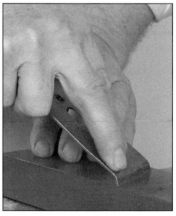

Dub off the sharp edge by lifting the back end of the cap iron.

Take the sharp corners off the long edges of a bench chisel, so it won't slice your fingers.

CHAPTER 8

Sharpening plane blades

A plane blade is the best tool for learning how to sharpen. The skill of sharpening is a chain with five links that begins only after the back of the blade has been flattened, and the edge has been shaped by grinding.

Learn each link in the sharpening chain in turn, then put them together to acquire the complete skill. The photos on these pages are keyed to right-handed people. If you are left handed, reverse the directions.

The five links in the sharpening chain are:

Grip

Stance

Angle

Motion

Pressure

The sharpening process

Each of these five links applies throughout the sharpening process. Once the plane blade has been ground, the sharpening process consists of three distinct steps:

1. Sharpen the 35-degree bevel on the medium (1200-grit) waterstone. This will raise a small burr.

2. Polish this sharpening bevel on the fine (6000-grit) waterstone. This will also remove the burr.

3. Back off, or polish, the back face of the blade on the fine waterstone.

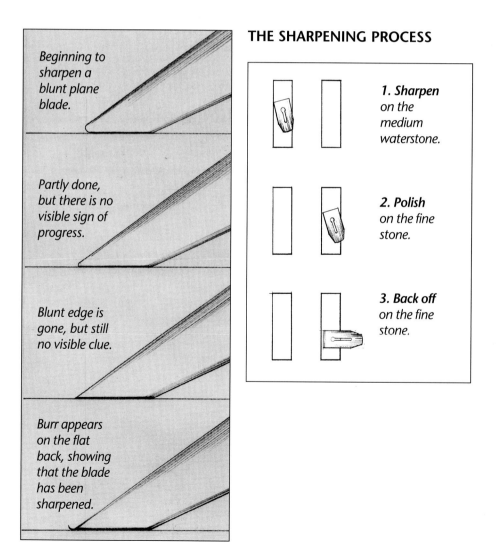

Beginning to sharpen a blunt plane blade.

Partly done, but there is no visible sign of progress.

Blunt edge is gone, but still no visible clue.

Burr appears on the flat back, showing that the blade has been sharpened.

THE SHARPENING PROCESS

1. Sharpen on the medium waterstone.

2. Polish on the fine stone.

3. Back off on the fine stone.

Grip

The grip is the first link in the chain.

The two-handed grip shown here gives you total control over angle, pressure and motion. With this grip you can vary the pressure across the width of the iron, to give it a slight curve, as explained on page 78.

Grip firmly, but not white-knuckles tight. The most common problem is gripping the blade too far away from the stone. This leaves too long a lever, which causes the blade to dig into the stone and gouge a piece out. Grip the blade as low and close to the stone as possible.

To learn the sharpening grip, follow these steps.

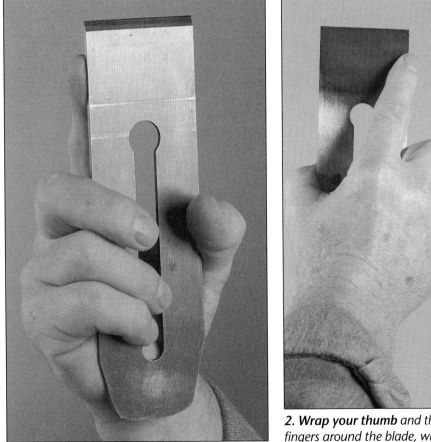

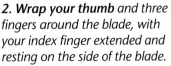

1. Grasp the blade in your right hand, with your index finger half over the edge. The bevel faces away from you.

2. Wrap your thumb and three fingers around the blade, with your index finger extended and resting on the side of the blade.

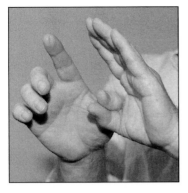

3. Now put the blade down. *The thumb of your left hand has to hook onto your right thumb. Try it without the plane blade, so you can see how to connect your thumbs.*

4. Then pick up *the plane blade in your right hand, as before. Link your two thumbs.*

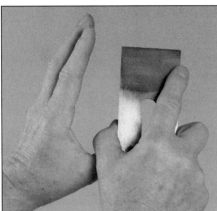

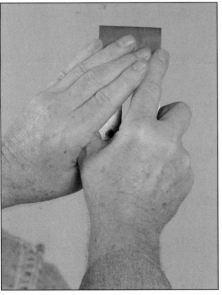

5. Pivot your left hand *so the fingers fan across the blade. Your little finger sits firmly on the edge of the blade.*

6. This grip *gives you total control over angle and pressure.*

Stance

Stance is the second link in the chain

A comfortable and relaxed stance positions your shoulders directly over the work. Your arms should be slightly bent. This stance lets your arms move so the blade remains at a constant angle while you apply controlled pressure at the same time.

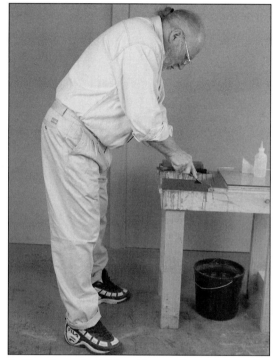

1. Stand comfortably with your feet apart and your knees slightly bent. When you lean forward to put the blade on the stone, you'll find yourself looking straight down on it. Don't tighten up. If your posture feels unnatural in any way, you don't yet have it right. Step back and try it again.

2. The sharpening motion comes from your shoulders, not from your wrists or elbows. Your head and feet remain in the same place as you work the blade back and forth on the stone.

3. Keep the cutting edge square to the long edges of the stone. A few degrees of skew is not a problem, but turning the blade sideways weakens the metal by causing score marks parallel to the edge itself.

Angle

Angle is the third link in the chain

The nominal sharpening angle is 35 degrees. Consistency is more important than angular precision; there's a fuller discussion of angles on page 80. A simple wooden block finds the angle, and tells your muscles where it is. The block works as well as an expensive angle jig.

*1. **The sharpening angle** is 35 degrees. To learn where that is, make yourself a wooden gauge, a little block sawn at 35 degrees. Fit the gauge between the blade and the stone, and let your body feel the angle.*

*2. **Now remove the block.** Remove it with your right hand. Hold the blade at the sharpening angle with your left thumb and fingers.*

*3. **Bring your right hand** back into place. With the blade resting on the stone, and with your left thumb as the fulcrum, it's easy to maintain the angle. Your own left hand is your own built-in honing guide.*

Motion

Motion is the fourth link in the chain

Move the blade from one end of the stone to the other, maintaining the angle established by the 35-degree block. Swing your arms from the shoulders, adjusting your muscles to maintain the angle. Concentrate on the setup and on how the blade moves over the stone.

Move back and forth in a straight line. A figure-eight motion merely adds an unnecessary complication. Use the full length of the stone, to delay wearing a hollow in the center and lengthen its working life.

Don't let the surface of the stone dry out. If it does, it will glaze over with swarf and lose its cutting power. Pause whenever there is no puddle of water atop the stone, and squirt it wet once again. A stone stored in water becomes thoroughly soaked, so water keeps squeezing out as you sharpen.

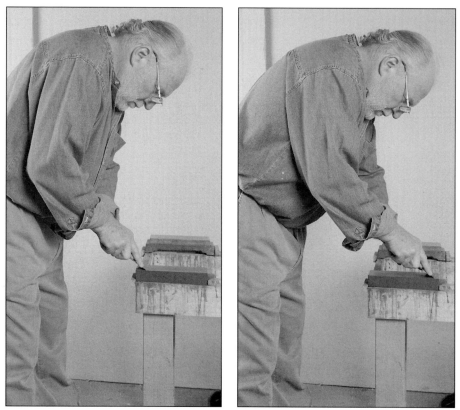

With the stones mounted on a low sharpening station, you can move your arms from the shoulders while maintaining the sharpening angle.

Pressure

Pressure is the fifth link in the sharpening chain

Because your body is above the action, you've got close control over the amount of pressure you can apply. Maintain a firm grip with light pressure until you get the feel of it, then increase the pressure on the forward stroke and relax it on the return stroke.

Because pressure is a function of grip, you will be able to feel the cutting action in your hands. If you press too hard and the plane blade digs into the stone, ease up a bit, and shift your grip closer to the edge. Control of pressure comes from experience. Every time you sharpen, concentrate on increasing the pressure up to your own comfort level.

When to stop

Sharpening on the medium waterstone will raise a minute burr on the back side of the plane blade. Stop and check with your fingers. You may not be able to see the burr, but you will be able to feel it.

Once it's there, stop and move over to the fine stone to polish the bevel and to back off. Move over with your feet but try to maintain every other part of the stance.

White knuckles. The sharpening grip gives you close control of pressure, and because your body is over the work, you can apply as much pressure as you can control without gouging the waterstone.

Curving the edge
Keep the corners from digging into the wood

All plane blades need to be minutely curved from side to side, across the cutting edge. Otherwise, the corners of the blade will dig into the wood, leaving a series of marks or tracks. Merely dubbing off the corners of the plane blade is not the answer. This only softens the corners of the plane tracks, which you will still be able to see and feel.

The obvious question is how much curvature. The answer depends upon how thick a shaving you intend to peel off the workpiece. Aim for a curve that is cutting 90% to 95% of its full width at the shaving thickness you want, creating a shaving that feathers to nothing on either side. Thick shavings require more curve than thin shavings.

To create the curve, apply pressure first on one side of the blade and then on the other, using the right index finger, and then the left little finger. Apply this side pressure for two or three strokes on the medium stone, then for eight to ten strokes on the fine stone. Hold a straight-edge up to the blade to check the results.

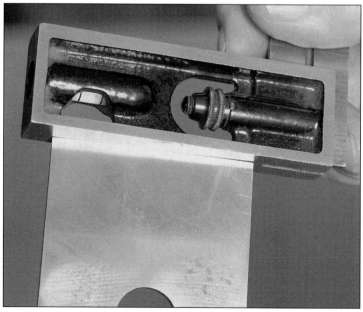

Curved edge. Increase the sharpening pressure toward one side and then the other, in order to create a curved edge. Check it by holding the blade against the stock of a try square.

CURVING THE EDGE

The sharp edge of the plane blade has to be curved, not straight.

A straight edge cuts a wide groove, leaving ridges called plane marks.

Rounding off the corners isn't a solution. All this does is make plane marks with rounded corners.

You should be able to cut a shaving with 90% to 95% of the blade's width. For a fine shaving, sharpen a slight curve into the blade, by bearing down harder on the edges. Thicker shavings call for more curve.

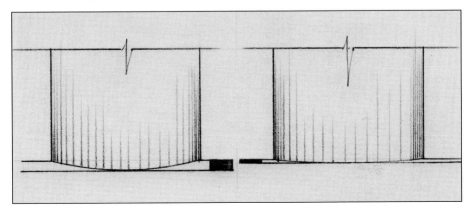

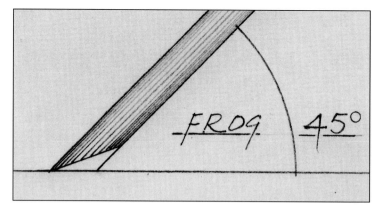

The plane's frog is fixed at a 45-degree angle to the sole. This geometry is why the plane blade has a grinding angle of 25 or 30 degrees and a sharpening angle of 35 degrees.

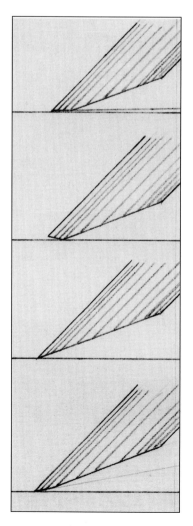

Because the frog of a bench plane is fixed at 45 degrees, a sharpening angle of 44 degrees is the absolute maximum. There would be 1 degree of clearance.

Sharpening at more than 45 degrees means the blade cannot cut, because its heel hits the wood.

There is no theoretical minimum sharpening angle. In practice, a sharper angle does not hold up in the wood. Here is a sharpening angle of 25 degrees. It would be fragile, and quick to chip.

The standard sharpening angle of 35 degrees, which has a clearance angle of 10 degrees, cuts well in normal hardwoods like cherry, maple and oak. To plane hard exotic woods, increase the angle by about 5 degrees.

Backing off

The last step in sharpening is to polish the back of the blade on the fine waterstone. This step removes any remaining traces of the sharpening burr. It also ensures that the back face of the blade is as bright and smooth as the sharpening bevel.

Backing off is a simple maneuver. Simply flip the blade onto its back face and move it up and down the stone under even pressure, keeping as much of the blade on the stone as you can fit. Make sure there's plenty of water on the stone. If a black skid-mark forms, the stone has begun to dry and the blade will stick at that point. Wipe the stone and squirt more water onto it before you continue.

Backing off. *Polishing the flat back face of the blade is the last step in the sharpening process. It takes only a few strokes on the fine stone.*

Block plane

The block plane blade is smaller than a regular plane blade, but exactly the same in every other way, so it is sharpened in the same way. Although there are regular and low-angle block planes, the sharpening angle doesn't change. It's 35 degrees, the same as the blade of a regular bench plane. The term "low angle" refers to the plane's frog, not to the blade itself.

You can grind a block plane blade with the same holder you use for a regular plane blade. The only necessary modification is an additional drilled hole to accommodate the smaller blade. However, if you have a lot of block planes, you can make a holder specifically for them.

Sharpen the block plane blade in exactly the same way as the blade of a regular bench plane.

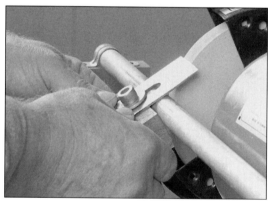

Grind the block plane blade using the regular plane blade holder.

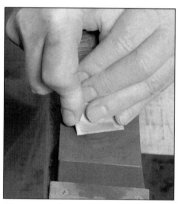

Sharpen the block plane blade exactly like a regular bench plane blade.

Block planes have low frogs, 17 degrees in this sketch. Despite the low frog, because the blade sits bevel up, it meets the wood at a high angle: 17 + 35 = 52 degrees.

A low-angle block plane has a 12-degree frog. With a 35-degree sharpening angle, the blade meets the wood at 47 degrees, 2 degrees more than a a regular bench plane.

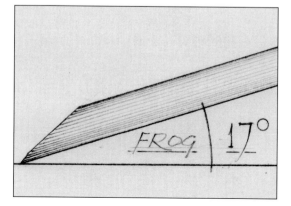

Spokeshave

The edge of a spokeshave blade has the same shape and angle as a regular place blade. However, the blade is too short to grind safely, and almost impossible to sharpen at a constant angle, unless you make a wooden holder for it. The drawing below shows one workable design, which handles both sharpening and grinding. Once you put the blade in a holder, the grip, stance and motion are the same as when sharpening planes and chisels. Take the blade out of the holder to back off.

It's a small point, but make the spokeshave blade holder about 1/16 inch narrower than the blade itself. This allows you to check the edge for squareness by indexing the square against the side of the blade.

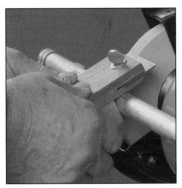

A wooden holder allows you to grind the spokeshave blade safely.

The holder also allows you to sharpen a short spokeshave blade just like a plane blade. The grip, stance and motion don't change.

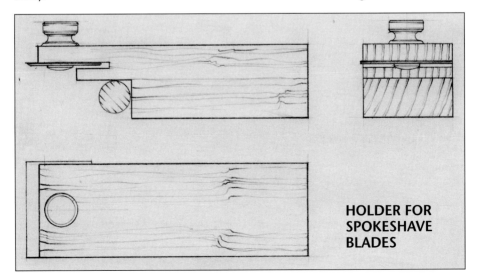

**HOLDER FOR
SPOKESHAVE
BLADES**

CHAPTER 9

Sharpening a chisel

In principle, sharpening a chisel is much the same as sharpening a plane blade. However, plane blades are wide and flat, easy to grasp and sharpen. Chisels vary all over the place, in both section and length, from carpenter's stubbies through cabinetmaker's bench chisels to heavy mortising chisels. Chisels are narrower than plane blades, which requires a different grip and more careful attention to pressure. And there is no need to vary the pressure across the width of the chisel, because you want a perfectly straight edge, without any curvature.

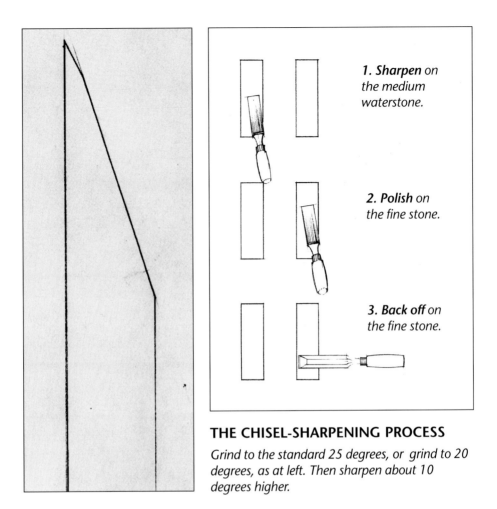

1. **Sharpen** on the medium waterstone.

2. **Polish** on the fine stone.

3. **Back off** on the fine stone.

THE CHISEL-SHARPENING PROCESS

Grind to the standard 25 degrees, or grind to 20 degrees, as at left. Then sharpen about 10 degrees higher.

The general sharpening procedure is the same for chisels as for plane blades:

Create or re-create the sharpening bevel on the 1200-grit waterstone.
Polish the sharpening bevel on the 4000-grit waterstone.
Polish the back face on the 4000-grit waterstone.

It's a common mistake to think that a small and narrow chisel will be a good blade for learning. A narrow chisel is the most awkward one to sharpen because you can't tell by feel whether or not it is sitting flat on the stone. It's also difficult to control the pressure, and easy to press too hard. Think of it this way: if it takes 40 pounds of pressure to sharpen a 2-inch plane blade, you'll only need 5 pounds on a 1/4-inch chisel, and half of that on a 1/8-inch chisel. Start with a wide chisel. Make learning easier by shortening the stroke.

Grip

The left thumb is the tool rest

Since chisels are smaller than plane blades, there isn't room for the full two-handed grip. Begin by bracing the chisel in the left hand. Extend the left thumb as a fulcrum, as shown in the photo at left. The left hand maintains the angle. The right hand stabilizes the tool and controls the pressure.

It's critical to grip the chisel close to its edge. If your hands are too far away from the surface of the stone, you're almost certain to dig the chisel into it.

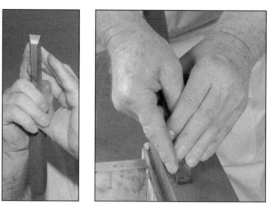

Two-handed grip: Position the left middle finger on the back of the blade, with the thumb underneath it.

Extend the right index finger along the blade, while wrapping the right thumb and remaining fingers around it.

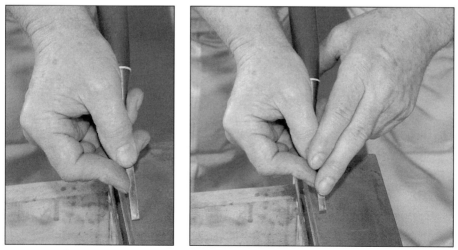

A narrow chisel is easier to grasp with the right hand, then insert the left. The left thumb goes under the blade or handle, with the middle finger on top.

Stance

Stand easy and relaxed

Chisel or plane iron, the stance is the same. The key is to position your body right over the stone, because this is the only way to maintain a consistent angle. Because small chisels require such a light touch, it's important to stand easy and relaxed, not hunched over and tense.

Some people turn the stone on edge to sharpen narrow chisels. The trouble with this practice is, it raises the height of the stone, which forces you to revise your carefully learned sharpening stance. As a result, it's more difficult to maintain the correct angle. It's better to leave the stone down flat, and at the right height for your body.

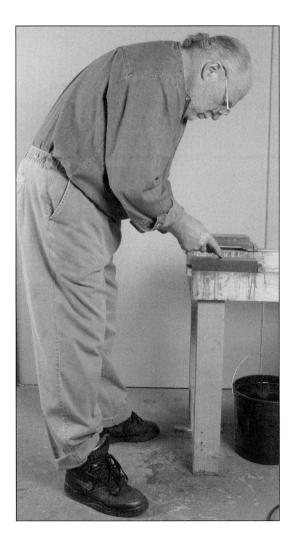

Take a relaxed stance, with your body directly over the sharpening stone.

Angle

Sharpen at a low angle

A chisel is a hand-guided tool, whereas a plane is a jigged apparatus. This allows you to be more personal about how you grind and sharpen your chisels. They can be ground as low as 18 degrees, which extends the length of the grinding bevel. A low angle not only gives you a better view of the work, it's also more elegant. The sharpening angle has to be 5 to 10 degrees higher than the grinding angle. While you could sharpen at a lower angle, the edge would be fragile. The higher the angle, the more durable the edge. I recommend a sharpening angle of 30 degrees.

Make a gauge block at the sharpening angle you want. Use the block to drop your hands into the right position for sharpening chisels.

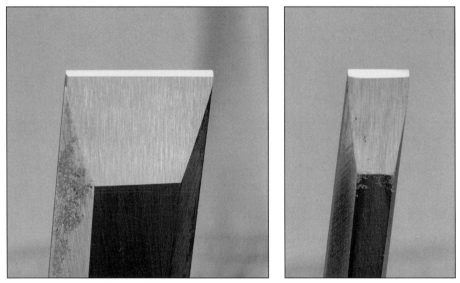

Perfect edge. *Correctly sharpened chisels have a long, clean grinding bevel with a narrow sharpening bevel that is so smooth and shiny it gleams. The sharpening bevel should be of uniform width across the chisel.*

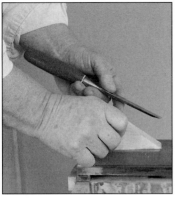

Begin sharpening by placing the 30-degree gauge block on the stone.

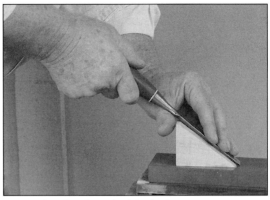

Plant the chisel on the block, then position your left hand. Thumb under the blade, fingers ranged along its back.

Hold the angle with your left hand, then remove the block with your right.

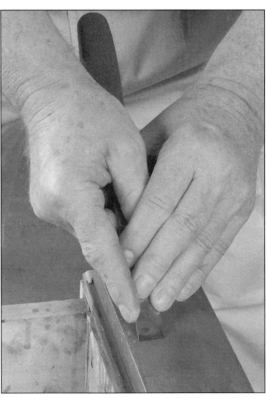

Slide your right hand into position, index finger extended alongside the chisel, thumb on top.

A stubby chisel may need a sawed-off gauge block. Otherwise, the grip is the same.

Pressure
Easy does it with chisels

Because a chisel is narrower than a plane blade, it takes less pressure to produce the same sharpening effect. The pressure comes from the fingers of the left hand, with the right hand offering stability and compensating for any tendency to tilt. Because a chisel is narrower than a plane blade, it's difficult to feel when the blade is truly parallel to the surface of the stone. You have to pause and look at the edge to make sure you're not inadvertently skewing the sharpening bevel. Pay attention to the back face of the chisel between your fingers and you'll be able to see when it is parallel to the stone.

Motion
Try a short stroke

The sharpening motion varies according to the width of the chisel. Chisels wider than an inch can be sharpened like plane blades, using the full length of the stone. Sharpen in a straight line, not in a figure 8. Try to use the edges of the stone's broad surface instead of its center.

Narrow chisels, 1/2 inch and smaller, are difficult to work over the whole surface of the stone. Instead, use one end or the other, and make short strokes of 3 inches to 4 inches. It's most important to keep the edge square and to maintain the angle. It's less important to worry about wearing the stone unevenly — which you won't do anyway, because sharpening a chisel requires so much less pressure than a plane blade.

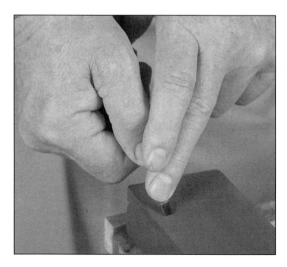

Sharpen narrow chisels with a short stroke at one end of the stone.

Backing off

Polish the flat back face of the chisel

Create the sharpening bevel on the medium waterstone. Work the bevel until you raise a burr on the back face, then move to the fine stone to polish the sharpening bevel. This will remove most of the burr, but you'll still need to flip the chisel over and polish the back of the blade, also on the fine stone.

Backing off takes hardly any time, though it's worthwhile to spend a little longer than is strictly necessary. Bit by bit, you'll polish and refine the back face, steadily improving your chisels.

Backing off. Lay the blade flat on the stone, but put the most pressure right at the cutting edge. Work the blade from one end of the stone to the other.

Backing off polishes the flat back face right at the cutting edge. Bit by bit this process extends the polish farther up the chisel.

CHAPTER 10

Knives and scissors

Sharpening plane blades and chisels gives you a good understanding of the geometry of a sharp edge. When you encounter tools that aren't strictly for woodworking, like pocket knives, kitchen knives and scissors, you should begin by taking a close look at the cross-section of the blade. The task of sharpening is to recreate the original geometry, then to give the edge the same qualities that any sharp edge must have: two smooth and polished metal surfaces, meeting at a controlled angle.

Pocket knives and marking knives

The shoulder lines of most woodworking joints are laid out with the layout lines. A clean line is essential for making the joint. Once the parts have been glued together, the layout line is all that remains visible on the surface of the wood. That's why you need a good marking knife. After trying all of the alternatives, I've settled on an ordinary Swiss army knife. It's made of good steel, it's stiff and won't collapse. It fits your hand, so you can bear down to make a deep line. It's good for cutting veneers and also for whittling, as well as for marking. It does a superb job without any fuss.

You may be tempted by the sharpness of an Xacto knife, a Stanley utility knife, or some other kind of disposable-blade tool. These knives are indeed sharp, but too thin and flexible for accurate layout.

A pocket knife rarely if ever needs grinding. If it's badly nicked, reshape the blade on the coarse waterstone. Then move through the medium and fine stones to refine and polish the cutting edge.

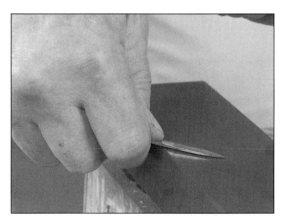

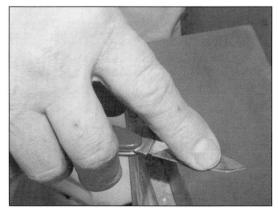

Hold the pocket knife flat on the stone, then tilt its back edge up a tad. Sharpen both sides of the blade in the same way.

Lay the blade flat on the stone, then lift it a bare 1/8 inch at the back edge. This will give it all the bevel it needs. Sharpen it the same on both sides. Don't press too hard to begin, and angle the blade with respect to the long edge of the stone. This helps keep it from closing on your fingers.

There's one situation when it is necessary to reshape the knife blade by grinding. Repeated sharpening is liable to make the knife point protrude when the blade is closed, as shown in the drawing at below. A protruding point is liable to slice your pocket and your finger. So, regrind the top edge of the blade so the tip lands inside the handle when the knife is closed.

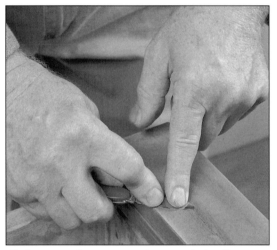

To increase the pressure, lay your index finger on the blade.

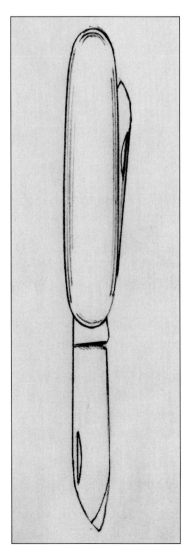

Repeated sharpening shifts the point of the knife so it protrudes dangerously when closed. It's necessary to reshape the blade by grinding.

Kitchen knives

Sharpen small kitchen knives the same way as small marking knives: almost flat on the waterstones. Don't try to grind them. Instead, visit the coarse waterstone when you want to re-shape the edge, then refine it on the medium and fine stones. Use the fingers of both hands to exert pressure from one end of the blade to the other, and move it sideways as well as back and forth.

You can bring large knives to the sharpening stone in the same way as small knives. However, many styles of knife, such as ham knives, are longer than the waterstones and they also flex easily. It's better to brace the knife in one position and take the stone to it. Hold the stone at a very small angle to the blade, about 3 degrees. Work the stone from one end of the knife to the other, taking long, smooth strokes, and do about the same amount of sharpening on both sides of the blade. If you work through the grits from coarse to fine, you'll be able to achieve scalpel sharpness.

Use both hands to exert pressure all along the blade of a kitchen knife. Move the blade sideways across the stone at the same time as you work it back and forth.

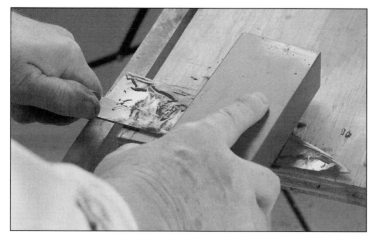

With large knives, it's easier to brace the knife on the sharpening table, while you move the stone.

Scissors

Scissors have the reputation of being difficult to sharpen but they are not hard to do. It helps to take them apart and sharpen each blade separately. This way you can work easily on all of one edge without interference by the other. However, the connecting screw is likely to be burred over like a rivet, preventing its removal. If the screw has become sloppy so the blades are not held in close contact with one another, use a ball-pein hammer to tighten it.

Hold the scissors blade in a vise — a metalworking vise does the job best — and bring the stone to it. Look at the existing profile and maintain it. Hold the stone in two hands, same as the file. The left hand is vital for maintaining the angle. Work through the coarse and medium stones, but stop at 1200 grit. There's no need to hit the finest stone.

Treat the inside faces of the blades like the flat face of a chisel or plane. Normally it's hollow ground, but it takes special equipment to maintain the shape. Back off with the blade flat on the stone, or else lay the scissor flat on the sharpening station and polish the inside face with a small slip.

Really beat up scissors can be straightened with a fine 6-inch flat file, then sharpened with waterstones.

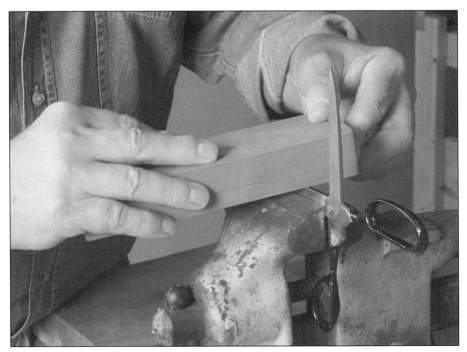

Hold the scissors in a metalworking vise and sharpen one blade at a time. Use the waterstone like a file.

Take a close look at the original bevel, then work carefully to not change it.

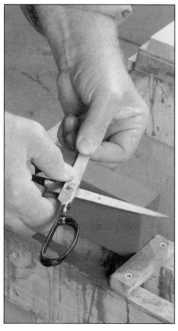

The inside of the scissors corresponds to the back face of a chisel or plane blade. Polish it on the edge of the stone, or else use a small slip.

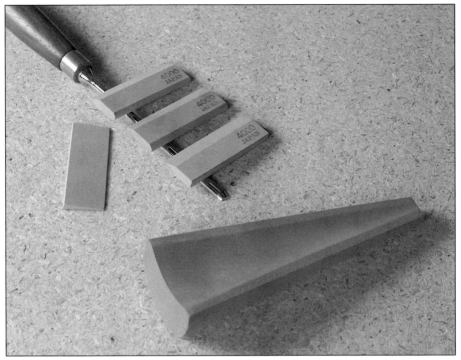

To sharpen carving tools, in addition to a grinder and flat waterstones, you'll need a collection of slip stones.

CHAPTER 11

Carving tools

There is no limit to the variety of shapes and surfaces to be carved, and there seems to be no limit to the different shapes of carving tools.

As with other woodworking tools, sharpening carving tools is a two-stage process. First you shape the edge and create the bevel on the grinding wheel. Then you sharpen the edge, and polish the metal, using sharpening stones. You can sharpen many times between bouts at the grinding wheel.

Carving tools do not have a flat bevel. They are sharpened with a rounded face, which allows them to ride into or cut their way out of the wood. Unlike bench chisels, which are sharpened with a flat back face in order to cut flat surfaces on the wood, carving tools are not self-jigging. While the bevel on most carving tools is on the outside face (out-cannel), some have it on the inside (in-cannel). Either way, the opposite face should be flat. There's no good reason to divide the bevel between the two faces.

Not only is the bevel rounded, but the cutting edge of most carving tools curves in at least one direction. Although you can shape the outside curve of most carving tools on a regular grinding wheel and a flat waterstone, you'll soon need a shaped wheel and a number of shaped stones, called slips, to match the shapes of various tools.

The match is only more or less. It's not practical to have a wheel or a stone for every tool in the carving kit. Instead, you work within a range of shapes to get the results you want. For a given curve a stone may work well, while for a smaller or tighter curve it just barely does the job.

Many carvers do all their sharpening on a hard felt buffing wheel charged with rouge or a similar polishing compound. The wheel conforms somewhat to the shape of the steel. Buffing is not as controllable as conventional grinding and sharpening, but when done slowly and gently, it does produce excellent edges.

In the end it's results that count, and the objective in sharpening carving tools is the same as regular woodworking chisels. You want an included angle of 20 to 25 degrees between the inside and outside surfaces, with the metal polished smooth and bright on both sides, right up to the cutting edge.

Section through in-cannel and out-cannel gouge.

Grind carving tools *in batches, not one at a time. Sit on a sawhorse or stool, and get comfortable, so you can concentrate on maintaining the grinding angle as you roll the tool along the rest.*

Grinding wheels

Most carving tools can be ground on a regular wheel. The general method is the same as grinding straight chisels and plane irons: first, reshape the edge by grinding straight into the wheel, then grind the bevel on the outside face of the tool. Since most carving tools are not flat, you can't use a holder. You have to roll them or pivot them freehand on the tool rest. You'll see exactly how to manage each type of carving tool on the following pages.

Tools with the grinding bevel applied to a concave face cannot be ground on a regular wheel. However, since cool-running wheels have a soft bond, it's easy to shape them. If you do a lot of carving, you'll probably want to shape a number of grinding wheels to suit the various types of chisel in your collection. For example, although a gouge can be ground on a standard, flat-faced wheel, if you carve a lot you may want to shape a wheel with a hollow face specifically for gouges. No carver owns every shape of chisel, but most collections contain four or five basic groups, each sufficiently different that you could end up with four or five different grinding wheels. Generally you'll be able to get a couple of shapes on a wheel, one on each edge.

Shape the wheels with a carborundum stick or a diamond dresser, same as you true the face of a flat wheel (page 43). The diamond dresser will take off material at a very rapid pace, so you can re-shape a wheel any time you need something different.

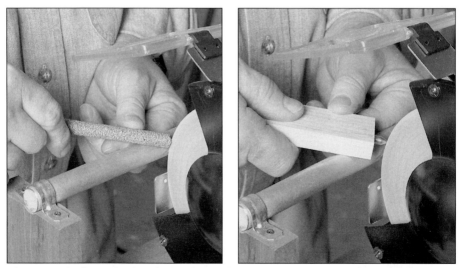

Shape a grinding wheel with a carborundum stick, or with a diamond dresser (right). This dresser has been mounted in a hole drilled in the end of a wooden block.

Slip stones

Small, hand-held sharpening stones, called slips, can be bought in various sizes and three basic shapes, as shown in the photo on page 98. As an alternative, ordinary flat water-stones can be shaped like slips to suit the tools in your kit. It's quick to do with coarse wet-dry paper, and it's a good way to get more mileage out of waterstones that have worn down thin, or that have been broken. You can put four different radii on the long corners of a stone, and four to six differently curved valleys along its faces and edges. Nevertheless, if you go this route and you do a lot of carving, you'll soon have a substantial investment in shaped stones.

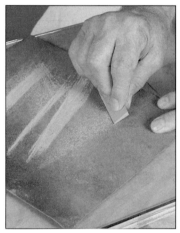

Reshape a slip to match the carving tool by working it across coarse wet-dry paper.

A regular waterstone can be reshaped to suit large carving tools. You can put four or even more shapes on its various edges.

The shaped waterstone fits the inside of the gouge.

Carving gouge

Gouges, or sweeps, are the most common general-purpose carving tool for removing material and roughing out shapes, and they're also the most straightforward to sharpen.

The edge of the gouge should be sharpened straight across and square to the tool's long axis. Experienced carvers may develop reasons for shaping the edge in some other way, and of course you can do what you like, but without experience telling you to do otherwise, grind the tool straight across.

Straighten the edge

Repeated sharpening is likely to distort the shape of the edge, by dubbing off the corners, dishing the center, or going out of square. Cutting into metal in the wood, or dropping the tool onto cement, is liable to nick the edge. The first step in sharpening is to inspect the edge closely and check it against the stock of a square. If it's not right, restore it by pushing it straight into the grinding wheel while simultaneously rolling it on the tool rest.

Use a square to check the edge of the gouge. It should be straight across.

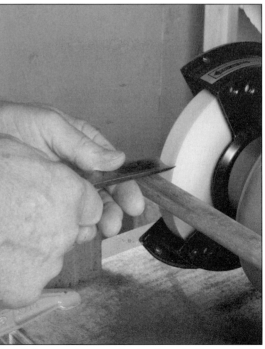

Straighten a damaged edge by grinding straight into the wheel. Press with your thumb to roll the tool on the rest.

Grind the bevel

While you could devise a jig to hold carving tools at the grinder, they are so various in shape that the best jig is your hands. Hold the gouge as shown in the photographs, bracing your index finger against the tool rest. Use your left thumb to control the rolling of the tool on the rest, as you roll the whole bevel across the face of the grinding wheel. Grind until the bevel is uniform and straight, and extends across the full width of the edge.

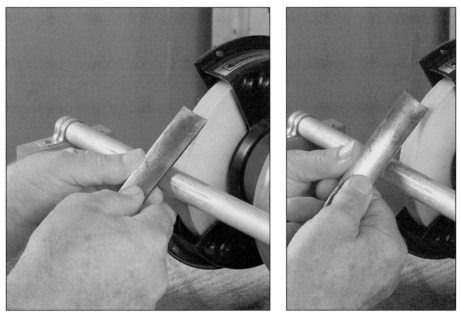

Jig the gouge with your fingers, and roll it on the tool rest to grind the entire surface of the bevel.

Sharpen the edge

Sharpen the outside of the gouge on a flat stone. Hold the gouge and maintain the sharpening angle with your right hand, as shown. Use the fingers of your left hand to push the gouge in a straight line across the stone, and simultaneously to roll the edge as it travels. Roll the edge in the opposite direction to the movement of the gouge across the stone. This way the entire sharpening bevel will come in contact with the stone.

Clean up the inside of the gouge with a conical slip, or with the shaped edge of a regular waterstone. The objective here is to polish the edge and remove any burr, but not to put any bevel on the inside of the edge.

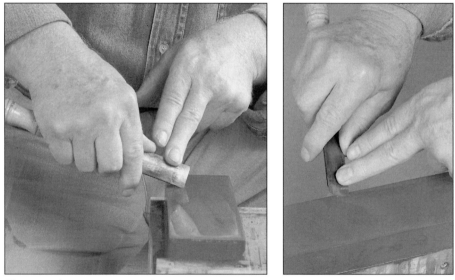

Sharpen the gouge on regular waterstones. Push the tool from one end of the stone to the other, simultaneously rolling the bevel.

Sharpen the inside bevel with a conical slip, or else with the shaped edge of a regular waterstone.

Spoons and bents

Grinding a spoon or bent gouge is the same as grinding a regular gouge, except it may require a little experimenting to find a comfortable grip. Be sure you plant the back or shaft of the tool on the tool rest, and brace the back of your fingers against the rest. Grind with a light touch, and roll the tool as you go.

Sharpen the tool same as a regular gouge, by rolling as you move it across the surface of the stone. When you deburr and polish the inside surface with a straight slip, you'll have difficulty avoiding the creation of a small bevel. You can either use the very tip of the slip and let it be good enough, or you can shape a stone to match the shape of the spoon.

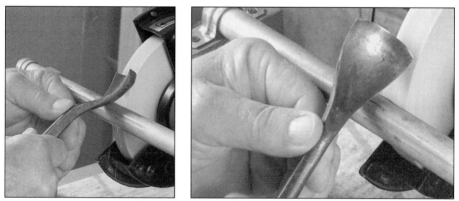

To grind the spoon, brace the back of your left hand against the tool rest and roll the shank of the spoon between your fingers and thumb.

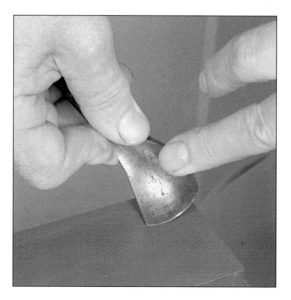

To sharpen the spoon, grasp the shank in one hand and push the bowl with the other. roll the spoon as you move it across the surface of the stone.

Deep gouge

Sharpen a deep gouge the same as a broad sweep. If the edge isn't straight across, begin by grinding it straight, then grind the bevel and sharpen the gouge by rolling it as you move it across the stone.

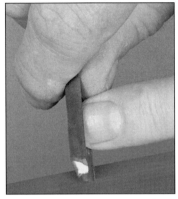

Maintain the angle of the deep gouge with one hand as you push it across the stone with the fingers of your other hand. Roll the gouge against the direction of travel.

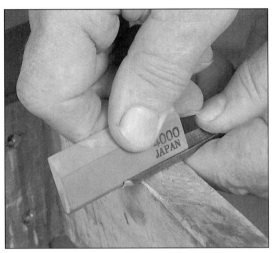

Shape the inside bevel and polish the metal with a small slip. Brace the deep gouge on the rail of the sharpening station.

Vee tool

The carver's vee tool is perhaps the most difficult to sharpen. It's all too easy to grind the base of the vee shape back too far, or to hollow the edge just above the point. The wings of the vee should make a right angle with the axis of the tool, and the cutting edges should be straight and smooth, meeting in a sharp point.

To restore a damaged vee tool, treat it the same as the other carving tools. First grind the edge to restore the geometry, then grind the outside of the tool to re-establish a bevel. Sharpen the outside faces on the flat waterstone, and finally clean up the inside with a slip shaped a few degrees sharper than the vee itself. The shaped slip allows you to sharpen one wing of the vee at a time, without affecting the other wing.

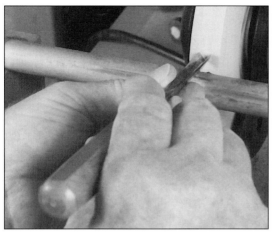

Reshape the cutting edges of the vee tool by grinding straight across. Grind all the distortion out of the edge.

Sharpen each outside face on a flat stone, just as if it was a regular chisel.

Polish the inside surfaces with a small shaped slip stone.

Veiner

Small, tight gouges, or veiners, can be sharpened on flat stones or on the felt buff, but the inside will have to be refined and polished with slip stones. There's no other way. The edge of the veiner has to remain in a plane at right angles, more or less, to the top of the flute. This geometry allows the deepest part of the veiner to enter the wood first, followed by the near-vertical sides. Pay attention to the geometry when grinding or sharpening the tool, because it's easy to cut the deep portion back too far. If you've got a veiner that can't make a clean cut, this is the probable problem. The solution is to grind it back straight across, using the lightest possible touch because there is not much metal to remove. Then reshape the sharpening bevel on medium stones, remove the burr, and polish the bevels inside and out.

Oversharpened veiner has a deep hollow at the center of its edge. It has to be ground straight before it can be resharpened.

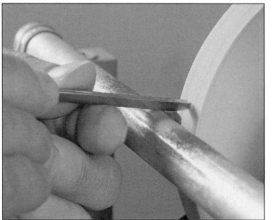

Straighten the edge by pushing the veiner straight into the wheel. Use a light touch to avoid overheating the steel.

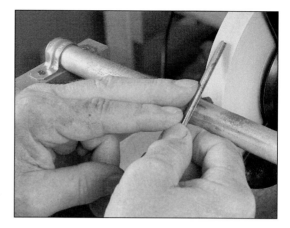

Roll the veiner on the tool rest to regrind the bevel.

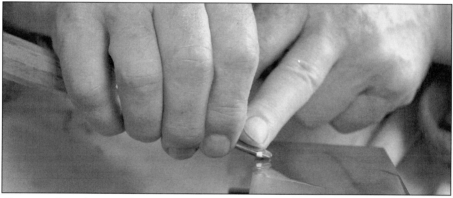

Sharpen the veiner on the waterstone. Maintain the angle with one hand, while pushing the tool with one finger of the other.

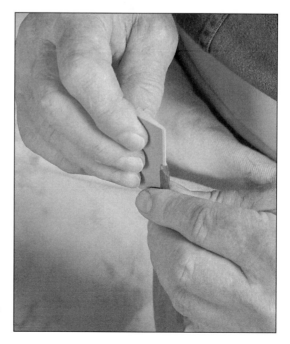

Polish the inside of the veiner with a small slip.

Buffing wheel

Many carvers prefer to shape and polish the edges of their tools on a cotton or hard felt buffing wheel charged with fine abrasive. The fabric conforms to the shape of the tools, and the abrasive is easy to replenish.

Note that unlike a grinding wheel, the buffing wheel must not be approached from the top. You have to use the underside of the tool rest, or else remove the rest and buff freehand, as shown below.

Like anything else, this method has advantages and disadvantages. On the plus side, the wheel easily merges the sharpening and grinding bevels into a smooth curve, which is what you want for carving. It's also a very quick method, and it produces a very sharp edge. On the minus side, it's easy to distort the cutting edge by attacking the wheel unevenly, and difficult to control he amount of metal being removed.

The buffing wheel can be mounted on a slow 1750-RPM bench grinder, or on a fast 3500 RPM machine, though given the choice I prefer the slower machine because it gives me more control.

The abrasive comes in the form of a block or a cylinder. It too can be purchased in several different degrees of fineness, but since you can't mix them on the wheel, it's best to choose one grade and stick with it. Most carvers get good results from red or green rouge.

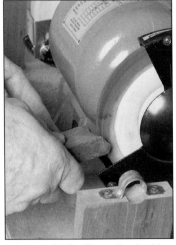

Charge the buffing wheel with a stick of rouge.

The buffing wheel conforms to the gouge. Remove the tool rest and work freehand on the underside of the wheel, never on the top side.

CHAPTER 12

Parting shot

A "skill" is nothing more than a learned habit, and that's what the art of sharpening amounts to: a set of habits you can learn. Once learned, like riding a bicycle, the skill is yours for life. And once you've got the skill of sharpening, your woodworking will change, because your planes and chisels will work in a way you've never before experienced.

Take your time and take it easy when you're trying to acquire this skill. When you know how, it takes only a minute to put a keen edge on a blade. While you're learning, don't spend more than three or four minutes on one blade. Stop, relax, take a walk around the shop. After you've acquired the skill, don't stand at the sharpening bench for more than 10 or 20 minutes. Even if you're sharpening a whole bundle of blades, do them in 10-minute stints with breaks in between.

When I'm working I don't like to stop to sharpen. And if I'm feeling pressed, I'll do a poor job of grinding and a lousy job of sharpening. So, I generally work with about 10 plane blades at a time, which allows me to pile them up for sharpening all at once. I can pick the right time, get out all the gear, and get into it.

It's not that sharpening a plane blade or a chisel takes a long time, it's that it isn't woodworking. You don't see any parts getting joined, glued or finished. So pick a time to grind and sharpen when that's the focus of the work. You can concentrate on this one thing, and the results will reflect your focus. And then you can get back to the work you really enjoy with tools and wood.

INDEX